HANDBOOK OF HEALTH & FITNESS

HANDBOOK OF HEALTH & FITNESS

Padmakshan Padmanabhan

Indus Source Books
Indian Spirit, Universal Wisdom

Indus Source Books
PO Box 6194
Malabar Hill PO
Mumbai 400 006
INDIA
Email: info@indussource.com
www.indussource.com

Handbook of Health & Fitness

ISBN: 978-81-88569-65-6

First published by Indus Source Books in 2014
First reprint 2017

Printed at Jayant Printery, Girgaum, Mumbai 400002

Contents

Preface

Modern sports scientists are relentlessly exploring new possibilities for excellence in every sports discipline and physical education.

As a result, the method of conducting physical education and sports training at all levels acquired much greater significance than ever before. Training methods have greatly advanced and enormous work has been done in the field, making the task of physical educators and coaches a bit easier.

This book will give an overall view of complete fitness, wellness, stress relief and yogic techniques to the training physical educators and sports coaches at various levels. This book deals with all aspects of wellness, fitness, exercises, nutrition, obesity, doping, sports injuries, yoga, recreational activities and also give an idea of some popular games.

It is necessary for a physical educator to take into consideration each of the above aspects which affect health and sports performance. I hope that it will prove to be a handy guide for coaches and physical educators as well as the sports &fitness enthusiasts and training physical educators aspiring to reach high level of training qualities.

Dr. KM Vasudevan Pillai
Chief Executive Officer
Mahatma Education Society

Introduction

One generally understands that the ultimate wealth of a human being is health. From a layman to an outstanding sportsman, health and fitness are the ultimate wealth to move on in life. In modern times spectacular improvement in human performance has been attributed mostly to modern methods and excellent knowledge of body mechanism.

People today are very aware of the importance of maintaining their physical health. Various means have been suggested as keys to improving one's well-being, but the fact of psychological stability is still too often downplayed, either because its importance is not fully recognised or there is no known way of strengthening the stability.

Today's fast moving world takes its own toll on the human body in the form of various kinds of stress that make people's lives miserable. Playing various sports for recreation or professionally, imparts key benefits to overcome stress.

High performing Athletes & Coaches today recognize that the most consistently effective methods of preparing for the demands of international competition are those based on proven scientific principles, rather than on trial and error. Sporting excellence is a very complex balancing act.

Adequate knowledge in all aspects of performance is necessary to get positive results. Positive thinking is very effective in sport. It can be allied with the phrases 'will to win' and 'playing to win'. All negatives have a positive somewhere, if you look hard enough. Sometimes people have great difficulty in finding a positive thought. All it takes is a helping hand from a coach or a mentor and the adequate knowledge will come into play.

I am sure that this book will give a helping hand to all physical educators and coaches who are training sportsmen/ physical educators, and health, fitness and sports enthusiasts in their day today activities.

Chapter I

PHYSICAL FITNESS AND ITS COMPONENTS

The term "fitness" is a word which is high on marketing in a busy, new world.

MEANING AND CONCEPT OF PHYSICAL FITNESS

Participating in physical activity is beneficial to people of all ages. Physical activity contributes to fitness, a state in which people's health characteristics and behaviour enhance the quality of their lives.

Physical fitness is defined as the ability of your body systems to work efficiently. A fit person is able to carry out the typical activities of living, such as work, and still have enough energy and vigour to respond to emergency situations and to enjoy leisure time activities. Physical fitness is a set of physical attributes related to a person's ability to perform physical activity successfully, without undue strain and with a margin of safety.

Physical Activity Meaning and Concept - The term physical activity describes many forms of movement, including activities that involve the large skeletal muscles. Activities that involve the small skeletal muscles (e.g. playing board games, drawing, andwriting) are important, but they do not provide the health benefits of activities that involve the large skeletal muscles and require substantial energy expenditure.

Health and Wellness Benefits of Physical Activity - Regular physical activity can do much to prevent disease and illness. It can help you look your best (with proper nutrition, good posture, and good body mechanics). Besides looking better, people who do regular physical activity feel better, do better at academic work, and are less depressed than people who are less active. Regular physical activity results in physical fitness which is the key to being able to do more of the things you want to do and enjoy life. It also allows you to be fit enough to meet emergencies and demanding day-to-day situations. Being physically active builds fitness which, in turn, provides you with many health and wellness benefits.

Physical activity is defined by its Duration, Intensity, and Frequency.

- Duration is the amount of time spent participating in a physical activity session.
- Intensity is the rate of energy expenditure
- Frequency is the number of physical activity sessions during a specific time period (e.g. one week).

TYPES OF PHYSICAL ACTIVITY

Physical activity suggests a wide variety of activities that promote health and well-being.

(I) Aerobic: light to vigorous-intensity physical activity that requires more oxygen than sedentary behaviour and thus promotes cardiovascular fitness and other health benefits (e.g.,jumping rope, biking, swimming, running, playing games like soccer, basketball, and volleyball).

(a) **Lifestyle:** physical activity typically performed on a routine basis which is usually light to moderate in intensity. (e.g., walking, climbing stairs, mowing the lawn or raking the yard)

(b) **Sports:** physical activity that involves competition, scorekeeping, rules, and an outcome that cannot be predetermined. There are two categories of sports - individual and team.

(II) **Anaerobic:** intense physical activity that is short in duration and requires a breakdown of energy sources in the absence of sufficient oxygen. Energy sources are replenished as an individual recovers from the activity. Anaerobic activity requires maximal performance during a brief period (e.g., sprinting while running, swimming or biking).

(a) **Physicalactivityplay:**playactivitythatrequiressubstantial energy expenditure but has flexible rules, usually self-selected, for the purpose of having fun (e.g., playing tag, jumping rope).

(b) **Weight-bearing:** physical activity that requires people to move their own weight.

MEANING AND CONCEPT OF EXERCISE

Exercise consists of activities that are planned and structured. It maintains or improves one or more of the components of physical fitness. Exercise is often associated with fitness maintenance or improvement only.

TYPES OF EXERCISE

Calisthenics: Isotonic muscle-fitness exercise that overloads muscles by forcing the muscles to work at a higher level than usual. Also called general PT exercises

Isokinetic: Muscle-fitness exercise in which the amount of force equals the amount of resistance, so that no movement occurs. Isokinetic exercise is an exercise that provides a variable resistance to constant limb movement. These kinds of adaptive exercises require equipment that can quickly accommodate changes in resistance. Isokinetic exercise is a form of active exercise in which a muscle or group of muscles contracts against a controlled, accommodating resistance which is moving at a constant angular velocity. The isokinetic exercises are performed with a specialized apparatus that provides variable resistance to a movement, so that no matter how much effort is exerted, the movement takes place at a constant speed. The isokinetic devices are computerized training and testing devices that provide maximum resistance through the entire ROM. The device provides multi-angle isometric resistance, resisted concentric and eccentric exercise.

Isotonic: Muscle-fitness exercise in which the amount of force exerted is constant throughout the range of motion, including muscle shortening (concentric contractions), and muscle lengthening (eccentric contractions). In an isotonic contraction, tension remains unchanged and the muscle's length changes. Lifting an object at a constant speed is an example of isotonic contractions. A near isotonic contraction is known as an auxotonic contraction.

There are two types of isotonic contractions: (1) concentric and (2) eccentric. In a concentric contraction, the muscle tension rises to meet the resistance, and then remains the same as the muscle shortens. In eccentric, the muscle lengthens due to the resistance being greater than the force the muscle is producing.

Isometric Resisted Exercise: Isometric resisted exercise is a static contraction of muscle against external resistance without appreciable change in its length or joint motion.

Advantage of Isometric exercise is valuable when joint motion is uncomfortable or contraindicated, during immobilization.

Isometric exercise is effective when weakness exists at a specific point in the ROM. The disadvantage of Isometric strength is specific to the joint angle. In other words, it is joint angle dependent.

Flexibility (Stretching): Exercises designed to stretch muscles and tendons to increase joint flexibility or range of motion. Specific flexibility exercises need to be done for each part of the body.

Muscle-fitness: Exercises designed to build muscle strength and endurance by overloading the muscles; also called progressive resistance exercises (PRE). Common forms of muscle fitness exercise include isokinetic, isometric, and isotonic.

The effect of physical activity, fitness and exercise on the brain: Some studies have found that physical activity can enhance the human cognitive functions. In addition to this it has been shown to be neuro-protective in many neurodegenerative and neuromuscular diseases. It also reduces the risk of developing dementiaand some evidence suggests that frequent exercise may reverse alcohol-induced brain damage. There are several

possibilities as to why exercise is beneficial for the brain. It increases the blood and oxygen flow to the brain, increasing growth factors that help to create new nerve cells and promote synaptic plasticity, increasing chemicals in the brain that help cognition such as dopamine, glutamate, norepinephrine and serotonin. Physical activity is thought to have other beneficial effects related to cognition as it increases the level of nerve growth factors, which support the survival and growth of a number of neuronal cells.

COMPONENTS OF PHYSICAL FITNESS

One of the misconceptions in the sports world is that a sports person gets in shape by just playing or taking part in his/her chosen sport. If a stationary level of performance, consistent ability in executing a few limited skills is your goal, then engaging only in your sport will keep you there. However, if you want the utmost efficiency, consistent improvement and balanced abilities, sportsmen and women must participate in year round conditioning programs. Fitness is the ability to carry out daily tasks with vigour and alertness without undue fatigue. In other words being fit is central to our health and to our sense of well being. Health and fitness mean more than just the absence of illness.If we are healthy and fit then the physical, mental, cultural and social aspects of our lives are working together. The human body is an amazing piece of machinery, one that adapts to the stress we put it under. As long as we don't overly stress our body, it will adapt and strengthen itself to cope. If you run every day your legs will get stronger and your cardio respiratory system will become more efficient. Sport scientists have discovered the best ways to train and increase our fitness levels in each fitness component. Essentially, we do the exercise that most mimics the action and fitness components we want to train and improve. To increase swimming we swim, to increase strength we lift weights. Major Physical fitness components are given below:

GENERAL HEALTH	SPORTS SPECIFIC
Muscular Endurance	Co-Ordination Ability
Cardiovascular Endurance	Balance
Strength	Agility
Flexibility	Power
	Speed

Exercise scientists have identified nine components that comprise the definition of fitness. They are what they call the "Key Methods of Sports Conditioning".

1. **Strength:** the extent to which muscles can exert force by contracting against resistance (e.g. holding or restraining an object or person)

2. **Power:** the ability to exert maximum muscular contraction instantly in an explosive burst of movement. The two components of power are strength and speed. (e.g. Shot Put or a sprint start)

3. **Agility:** the ability to perform a series of explosive power movements in rapid succession in opposite directions (e.g. Zigzag running or cutting movements)

4. **Balance:** the ability to control the body's position, either stationary (e.g. a handstand or while moving (e.g. a gymnastics stunt)

5. **Flexibility:** the ability to achieve an extended range of motion without being impeded by excess tissue, i.e. fat or muscle (e.g. executing a leg split)

6. **Muscle Endurance:** a single muscle's ability to perform sustained work (e.g. rowing or cycling)

7. **Cardiovascular Endurance:** the heart's ability to deliver blood to working muscles and their ability to use it (e.g. running long distances)

8. **Speed:** Is the ability of a person to execute motor movements with high speed in the shortest period of time. It is equal to the distance covered per unit of time. the element of speed is involved in most athletic skills such as in sprint running, some skills of soccer, basketball, etc.

9. **Co-ordination:** the ability to integrate the above listed components so that effective movements are achieved

TESTING THE FITNESS COMPONENTS

TEST	FITNESS COMPONENT
Speed sit-ups(60 sec)	Muscular strength, Muscular endurance
Sit and reach	Flexibility
50 meter sprint	Speed
Standing broad jump	Muscular power, Maximum strength
Push-ups	Muscular endurance
1.6 Km Run	Aerobic capacity
Stroke stand	Balancing ability
Shuttle run	Agility
Alternate wall toss	Co-ordination ability
Grip strength	Maximum strength
Body mass index	Body composition
Beep test	Aerobic capacity, Muscular endurance

THE PARTS OF PHYSICAL FITNESS

(I) Health - Related Physical Fitness

(II) Skill - Related - Physical Fitness

(I) Health - Related Physical Fitness: The health and fitness levels needed to carry out daily activities with littl fatigue and still have energy for emergencies. **To have enough fitness for good health we need the following qualities :** Aerobic Capacity, Muscular Strength, Flexibility and Body Composition

(a) **Cardiovascular fitness:** the ability to exercise your entire body for long periods of time. It is the ability of the heart and lungs to supply oxygen through the blood to the muscles. This allows us to work for relatively long periods without becoming overtired

(b) **Strength:** the amount of force your muscles can produce. It is the ability of our muscles to exert a force. This involves maximum strength, muscular power and muscular endurance. It helps to protect joints from injury. Strength = Mass x Acceleration 1 RM (Maximum Strength)

(c) **Muscular endurance:** the ability to use your muscles many times without tiring. Strength Endurance (General Strength) Explosive strength (Speed Strength)

(d) **Flexibility:** the ability to use your joints fully through a wide range of motion. It is the ability to move our joints through their full range of movement. Ballistic Method (swinging) Slow stretch and hold Post Isometric

Types of flexibility:

Active: The ability to perform without any external help.

Passive : The ability to perform high amplitude movement with extended force with the help of a partner

Dynamic: The ability to do movements with larger amplitude, when the body is in motion.

Static: resistance of joint when stationary

General Flexibility: The ability to perform movement with high amplitude in the largest joints and in different directions. It is the total sum of flexibility of all joint regions especially hip, shoulder and trunk.

Special Flexibility: The ability to perform movement with high amplitude in those joints and direction which correspond to the demand to certain sports

(e) **Body fatness:** composition: The percentage of body weight that is made up of fat when compared to other body tissue, such as bone and muscle It is the capacity to carry the right amount of fat and muscle.

Body Types:

(a) Ectomorph - Lean and Thin

(b) Mesomorph - Muscular

(c) Endomorph - Fatty/Bulky

(II) Skill Related Physical Fitness: If you want to develop a high level of fitness to play competitive sport you need to develop your sport-related components of fitness.This is the level of physical fitness needed to take on the demands of regular sporting activities. Although we may be fit from a health point of view, we may not have the fitness required to play a sport. There are many types of sports and each has its own unique demands on the body.

Different sports require different parts of skill - related fitness. Many sports require several parts. For example, a skater might have good agility, but may not possess good power. Some people have a more natural ability in skill areas than others. Good health does not come from being good in skill- related fitness.

(a) **Muscular Power:** This is the ability to use strength quickly to produce an explosive effort. e.g. jumping or throwing a shot put.

(b) **Maximum Strength:** Is the ability to apply maximum force to an immovable object.

(c) **Muscular Endurance:** Is the ability to work the muscles very hard for a period of time.

(d) **Speed (Anaerobic Capacity):** This is the ability to get your body moving quickly. Speed activities are short events requiring rapid movement, such as 100m track events or 50m swimming.

(e) **Agility:** This is the ability to accelerate quickly, dodge, weave and turn. Agility is essential in most team sports for actions such as avoiding the opposition or falling over and recovering quickly.

(f) **Balance:** Is the ability to stay upright and in control of your body position when you are moving or stationary. Most sporting activities require balance.

(g) **Co-ordination:** Is the ability to time your movements so you can perform them smoothly and accurately. All activities require some sort of coordination.

(h) **Reaction Time:** Is the ability to respond to a stimulus quickly.

Requirement of component for various games:

Cardio Vascular: Football, Rugby, Tennis, Long Distance Running

Muscular Strength: Rugby, Weight Lifting

Muscular Endurance: Rowing, Swimming, Running, Tennis, Cricket

Flexibility: Gymnastics, Racket Sports, Running, Cricket, Rugby

Body Composition: Long Dist Runner (Ectomorph), Swimmer (Mesomorph), Sumo Wrestler (Endomorph)

Physical fitness is a general state of wellbeing that includes the energy to participate in physical activity and reduce the risk of developing health problems prematurely. Physical Fitness includes bone strength, muscular strength, cardiovascular fitness, fiexibility and metabolic fitness. It allows a person to accomplish the task of the day with little drain of energy. Overall fitness increases when you address the factors that affect physical fitness.

DEFINITION AND CONCEPT OF WELLNESS AND HOLISTIC HEALTH

Wellness:

Wellness has been defined as a dynamic process that is ever changing. The well person usually has some degree of illness and the ill person usually has some degree of wellness. Wellness further describes the health status. It allows health to be placed on a continuum from one's optimal level (wellness) to a maladaptive state (illness).

Concept of Wellness: This concept of a health continuum negates the idea that wellness and illness are opposite because theymay occur simultaneously in the same person in varying degrees. Dimensions of Wellness:

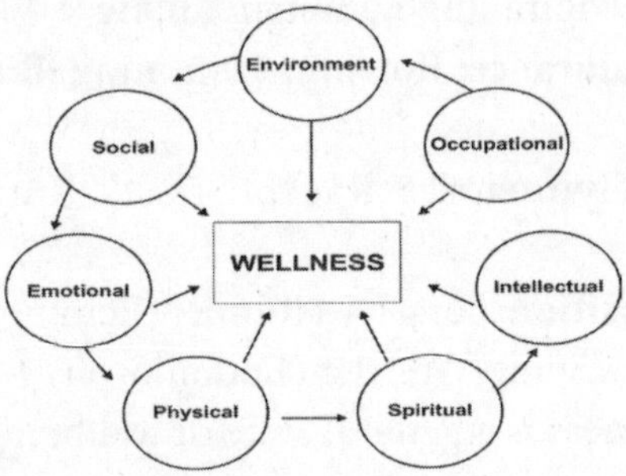

Health-Illness Continum

Measures a person's perceived level of wellness, health and illness/diseaseat opposite ends of a health continuum. Move back and forth within this continuum day to day. Wide ranges of health or illness.

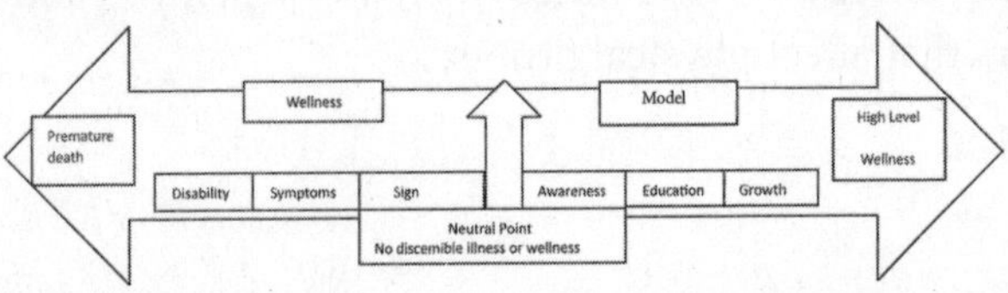

1. **Physical:** The ability to carry out daily tasks, achieve fitness (e.g. pulmonary, cardiovascular, gastrointestinal),

maintain adequate nutrition and proper body fat, avoid abusing drugs and alcohol or using tobacco products, and generally to practice positive lifestyle habits.

2. **Intellectual:** The ability to learn and use information effectively for personal, family, and career development.
3. **Social:** The ability to interact successfully with people and within the environment.
4. **Emotional:** The ability to manage stress and to express emotions appropriately. Emotional wellness involves the ability to recognize, accept, and express feelings.
5. **Spiritual:** The belief in some force (nature, science, religion, or a higher power) that serves to unite human beings and provide meaning and purpose of life.
6. **Occupational:** The ability to achieve a balance between work and leisure time, A person's beliefs about education, employment, and home influence personal satisfaction and relationships with others.
7. **Environmental:** The ability to promote health measures that improve the standard of living and quality of life in the community

Before concluding I also want you to understand what well being is. Well-being is a subjective perception of vitality (energy) and feeling well. It can be described objectively, experienced, and measured and it can be plotted (designed) on a continuum. Well-being is a component of health.

HOLISTIC HEALTH:

Holistic (holism) implies an approach or process which enables integration of multiple streams. Before we discuss holistic health we must understand what is health is. WHO describes health as a state of complete physical, mental, and social well-being and not merely the absence of disease or infirmity.

To understand health there is no consensus on any definition of health. There is knowledge of how to attain a certain level of health, but health itself cannot be measured.

Traditionally health has been defined in terms of the presence or absence of disease and some people define health as a state of being well and using every power the individual possesses to the fullest extent. Most people define health as being free from symptoms of disease and pain as much as possible; being able to be active and to do what they want to do or must do; being in good spirits most of the time.

The words "holism" and "holistic" are derived from the Greek word holos, meaning "whole". Holism is based on an understanding that the whole is greater than the sum of its parts.

The concept of holistic health is when one part of the body or mind is not working properly, it is believed to affect the whole person. Holistic approaches focus on the whole person rather than just on the illness or part of the body that is not healthy.

AN OVER VEIW OF PHYSICAL FITNESS

Throughout the physical training industry there are many myths, misconceptions, theories and principles on the different styles of fitness training. This concentrates on the six principles that govern physical fitness.

Overload: In order to improve, various fitness components the body needs to be stressed beyond what the body normally encounters. This increases both systematic (structured) and progressive (unstructured) programs to ensure performance gain without injuries. To get better results you must shock the system and place a higher demand on it than it is used to.

Recovery: Recovery is just as important as the hard work that you put into your training regime. There are several methods that may enhance the recovery phase. These are massage, hydro-therapy, yoga and reflexology all of which can help your body make the necessary repairs prior to moving onto the next training session.

Progression: The principle of progression in exercise emphasises that a person should start slowly and increase the exercise gradually. This will help avoid muscle soreness and minimise injuries. When structuring an exercise program ensure the following acronym is used to ensure progression. F - Frequency, I - Intensity, T -Time, T- Type of exercise.

Individuality: No two people are alike. Whether it be a gender difference, race difference or a genetic difference. When it comes to physical training we all have different requirements that need to be considered. Endomorph (larger) people may not recover as quickly or have the same aerobic capacity as ectomorph (thinner, smaller build) people. These individual differences need to be addressed when evaluating training programs.

Specificity: Is a principle in which specific kinds of exercise need to be used to develop specific parts of the body and specific elements of fitness.

Variety: "Variety is the spice of life". Well, it also applies to fitness training.

FACTORS AFFECTING PHYSICAL FITNESS

(1) Heredity (2) Body Type (3) Age (4) Gender (5) Diet (6) Health Status (7) Lifestyle

(1) **Heredity:** Our genetic make-up, in part, determines our physical potential and capabilities. At present, it is believed that physical ability is 75% genetic and 25% training and environment.

(2) **Body Type:** Although the structure of the body is almost the same for most individuals, body types do differ from individual to individual.

(a) Ectomorphs tend to be long boned and lean. These

individuals generally carry very little body fat or muscle bulk.

(b) Mesomorphs tend to be muscular and relatively well proportioned. These individuals generally gain muscle bulk easily.

(c) Endomorphs tend to be soft, well rounded with large proportions. These individuals generally gain body weight easily.

(3) Age: Age is no barrier to exercise although younger individuals are potentially more capable of achieving a higher level of fitness. However, it is important to note that the rate of decline associated with aging can be largely diminished with regular exercise.

(4) Gender: Over the years, the gaps in exercise performance between men and women have narrowed tremendously. However, some differences still remain. Women tend to be more flexible while men, potentially, have greater muscle strength

(5) Diet: Establishing healthy eating patterns will provide the body with the essential nutrients it needs to maintain itself and sustain physical activity. Exercise places extra demands on our energy sources and if not replenished will result in fatigue and poor physical performance.

(6) Health Status: Physical performance will be affected by poor health.

(7) Lifestyle: Healthy habits such as regular exercise, adequate and proper nutrition will have positive effects on physical fitness. On the other hand, less healthy habits such as smoking, high alcohol consumption and the use of recreational drugs will have an adverse effect.

FACTORS AFFECTING WELLNESS

There are two types of factors that affect wellness extensively -

(1) Internal Factors

(2) External Factors

Internal Factors: Biologic dimension, genetic makeup, sex, age, and developmental levels all significantly influence a person's health. Psychological dimension and emotional factors influencing health include mind-body interactions and self-concept. Cognitive dimensions include lifestyle choices and spiritual and religious beliefs.

External Factors: The environment, standards of living reflecting occupation, income, and education, family and cultural beliefs, patterns of daily living and lifestyle, including the upbringing of children, social support networks, friends, or confidants and job satisfaction. All of these help people avoid illness.

Illness and Disease: A highly personal state in which the person's physical, emotional, intellectual, social, developmental, or spiritual functioning is thought to be diminished. Illness is usually associated with disease but may occur independently of it. Illness is a highly personal state in which the person feels unhealthy or ill.

THE DIMENSIONS OF HEALTH AND WELLNESS

-IMPACT		IMPACT +
Depressed	Emotional Mental	Happy
Ignorant	Intellectual	Informed
Unfit	Physical	Fit
Lonely	Social	Involved
Unfulfilled	Spiritual	Fulfilled
Negative	Total Outlook	Positive

ACHIEVING WELLNESS

Wellness is the product of healthy lifestyles just like fitness is the product of regular exercise. Wellness reflects how one feels about life as well as one`s ability to function effectively.

OPTIMAL HEALTH MODEL

Freedom from diseases + Freedom from debilitation conditions >Wellness>Optimal Functioning+ Meaningful work contribution to the society>Wellness and quality of life

Priority lifestyles for good health are physical activity, nutrition and stress management. The reason why these lifestyles are especially critical is that they affect the lives of all people. Many can make improvements. Small changes can have a major impact on individual and public health.

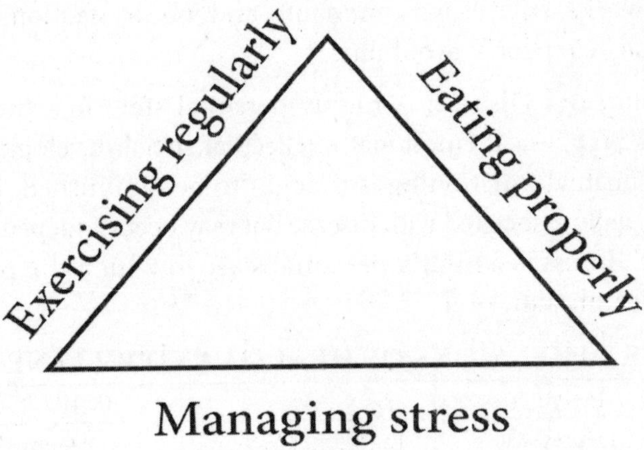

Chapter II

OBESITY, SPORTS INJURIES, NUTRITION AND DOPING

CONCEPT - TYPES AND CAUSES OF OBESITY AND ITS MANAGEMENT

The definition of obesity is a state of excess accumulation of fat tissues beyond the limitation of the skeletal and muscular requirement. Extra fat gets deposited gradually in (a)The surface layer of the heart (b) The loose tissues around the kidneys (c) The supporting tissues within the abdomen

The concept of obesity is that physically fit, obese patients have lower mortality rates than unfit, normal weight persons!. Being thin doesn't guarantee being healthy

Being fat doesn't have to be unhealthy.

Physical activity and cardiovascular fitness are much more predictive of health than body weight. Despite the protection against cardiovascular disease. and the all cause mortality that cardio-respiratory fitness incurs, obesity still has its problems.

Obesity is associated with increased risk of co-morbid conditions: Hypertension, Dyslipidaemia, Diabetes mellitus, Coronary artery disease.

Cerebrovascular disease. Overall mortality higher Gallbladder disease. Sleep apnoea

Osteoarthritis, Gout, Cancers (Colon, Breast, Prostate, Uterus, Cervix)

Before we study detailed obesity, one must know the body composition.

Body Mass Index (BMI) is the global method of determining overweight/obesity

BMI	=	Weight/Height^2 (kg/m^2)
Essential fat	=	Heart, Lungs, Kidney, Muscle, Female Sex Specific
Storage Fat	=	Subcutaneous
Lean body mass	=	Body Mass -Storage Fat mass 8.4 = 61.6 Kg)
Present Fat	=	Skinfold/Girth Measurement
Fat mass	=	% Storage fat / 100 x Body mass
Desirable Body mass	=	Lean Body Mass / 1 - Reduction fat %
Desirable fat loss	=	Body Weight - Desirable body mass
Body Mass	=	Body Weight in Kg / Height in meters Index square

Normal	:	BMI 18 - 24.9
Overweight	:	25 - 29.9
Obese	:	> 30
Class I	:	30 - 34.9
Class II	:	35 - 39.9
Class III	:	> 40

Causes of Obesity: The following are generally believed to be the causes of obesity (1) Getting minimum physical exercise (2) Eating pattern (3) Concept of obesity "the disease of the royal lifestyle (4) Mind over body (5) Too much food intake (6) Insufficient energy output (7) Not enough exercise (8) Low resting metabolic rate (9) Genetic predisposition (10) Environment favouring weight gain (11) Psychological stressors.

TYPES OF OBESITY:

(1) **Android Type:** also called "abdominal" or "central" obesity. This type people have an apple shape. Their shoulders, face, neck, chest and upper part of the abdomen are bloated. The stomach has a stiff appearance as do the shoulders and breast. The lower part of the body - the hips, thighs and legs are thinner and out of proportion compared to the upper part of the body. In these persons the vital organs affected will mostly be the heart, liver, kidney and lungs. Though this type of obesity is founded more in males, due to the modern life style and eating habits it is now fairly common in females also.

(2) **Gynaeoid Type**: also called "peripheral" obesity This type of people has a pear shape. The lower part of the body has extra flesh and iscommon to both sexes, though females are more affected.

The flesh is somewhat flabby in the abdomen, thighs, buttocks and legs. As these persons grow old the whole figure assumes a stooping posture and the spine will never be erect due to the heavy hips and thighs. The vital organs most affected are the kidney, uterus, intestines, bladder and bowels.

(3) **The Third Type:** Besides Android and Gynaeoid there is one more type of obesity. It is known as the third type. There are people, however, who do not belong to either of

the above types of obesity. Their whole body from head to toe looks like a barrel. Their gait is more rolling than walking.

Consequences of Obesity: Obesity is not a disease in itself but it is the root of many diseases like high blood pressure, heart trouble, diabetes, kidney trouble, gout, joint pain and skin diseases. Some of these increase the rate of mortality. The more a person's weight, the greater the chance of early death.

(i) **Dangerous to vital organs:** The fat deposits create an overload, the heart muscles can do nothing but over work during the process of supplying blood to the tissues, causing discomfort to the heart. The lungs purify the blood and send it back to the heart which then pumps it out to the rest of the body. Hence any hindrance in the heart's functions disrupts the lungs too.

(ii) **Muscle, Joint pain and Kidneys:** Excess weight interferes with skeletal muscular activities. All the weight bearing joints are burdened by excess weight. Rheumatism, Gout and Arthritis are common in people who are overweight. More fat tissues the body contains, the greater the task of elimination of wastes by the kidneys.So for an obese person, kidney disease tends to develop easily.

FACTS ON EXERCISE IN OBESITY:

Exercise alone only leads to a slight loss of weight, if any, but there is a marked reduction in the mortality rate. Adding moderate/vigorous aerobic exercise to dieting slightly increases weight loss. Aerobic exercise during weight loss lessens loss of Fat Free Mass (FFM). Resistance exercise during weight loss preserves FFM and may help maintain weight loss. Any type of exercise helps maintain weight loss, but its duration must be 4-10 hours/week. Compliance may be better with multiple short-bout sessions.

MANAGEMENT OF OBESITY

Behaviour modification strategies, extended treatment, and physical activity are excellent predictors of weight loss during treatment.

THE GOAL OF TREATMENT.

(1) Get patients to look like models? Absolutely not!!!
(2) Get patients to their ideal body weight? Not practical, usually
(3) Get patients to lose 5-10% of body weight? Yes, hopefully
(4) Get patients to exercise and reduce their mortality risk? Most definitely!

REASONABLE EXPECTATIONS FOR MANAGING OBESITY:

(a) Gradually develop regular exercise
(b) Gradually develop more healthy eating habits
(c) Aim to lose 5-10% of body weight first

WHY NOT LOFTIER GOALS?

(i) Rarely do obese patients achieve the ideal weight
(ii) Falling short of lofty goals, which is so common, leaves patients disappointed and highly susceptible to regain lost weight
(iii) Health can be achieved while still obese through the "Healthy Obesity" concept

Treating and managing obesity demands a multi-faceted approach with chronic monitoring.

1. **Decreased caloric intake:** 500-1000 kcal/day less than usual Lose 1-2 lbs/week Women: 1000 - 1200 kcal/ day total diet Men: 1200 - 1500 kcal/day total diet2.

2. **Increased exercise :** Exercise regularly Need to gradually work up to this Start with brisk walking 10-45 min, 3-5 days/week Work up to 60-80 min, most if not all days/ week Aim to expend 1,000 - 2,000 kcal/week

Understand what type of exercise is best for obesity treatment. The ideal may be a combination of aerobic and resistance training.

The Trainer has to counsel the obese person to increase exercise.

Use the 5 As of counselling:

(i) Address the agenda (ii) Assess the Knowledge, beliefs, concerns, feelings, stage of change (iii) Advise on personalized exercise recommendations (iv) Assist and provide support, identify barriers and resources (v) Arrange follow-up and see patient two weeks later and every month thereafter. When following up,

Ask about progress, Encourage!

Ask about barriers.

Discuss remedies.

Weigh the patient

Follow cholesterol, blood sugar, BP, etc.

Tailor counselling to the patient's stage of change:

(a) **Pre-contemplation** - not remotely interested: Provide handout on health benefits of weight loss and exercise. Discuss barriers to exercise

(b) **Contemplation** - considering weight loss

(c) **Preparation** - start making small changes: Give specific advice on FITT (Frequency, Intensity, Time and Type of exercise).

- **Frequency:** most if not all days of the week

- **Intensity:** 55-90% of max heart rate
- **Time:** 30-80 minutes: (a) Gradually work up to this
(b) Start with brisk walking 10 min, 3-5 days/week
(c) Work up to 60-80 min, most or all days of the week
- Type: aerobic, resistance

(d) **Action** - meeting behaviour change criteria
(e) **Maintenance** - steady behaviour over time

3. BEHAVIOURAL MODIFICATION:

(a) **Self-monitoring:** One of the most helpful tools in obesity management.

Observation and recording of behaviours like total calorie intake, fat grams consumed, food groups used, situations that promote overeating, amount/intensity of exercise, weight, body composition, etc. Provides patient objective feedback so improvements can be made.

(b) **Stimulus control:** Identifying and modifying the environmental cues that are overeating and inactivity. Laying workout clothes on the bed to increase the likelihood of exercise the next morning. Eating only at the kitchen table will help avoid situations where overeating is common.

(c) **Body image and self-esteem counselling:** Many obese patients have poor self-esteem - negative thoughts lead to poor compliance. Many people have unrealistic weight loss expectations - an ideal body weight instead of going for a 5-10% reduction. Obese people also have a distorted body image. As a result, about 20% of obese people wont exercise because they feel too fat.

(d) **Stress management:** Stress is a primary predictor of relapse and overeating.

Management techniques are very effective in obesity treatment. Refer to mental health professionals if you yourself are not skilled.

(e) **Social support:** Those who have social support will

have greater success. e.g. friends, family and community based groups like health clubs, education courses, weight watchers, church related activities, etc.

4. PHARMACOTHERAPY :

Candidates:	BMI 27 - 29.9 + risk factor BMI >30 Never use as the sole therapy Poor effectiveness Poor long term maintenance of weight loss Agents approved by FDA for long term use
Medicine:	Sibutramine:
Effect:	Appetite suppressant, thermo genic Proven efficacy, even after one year of medication Improves TC, LDL, TG, HbA1c
Side-effects:	Headache elevated BP, insomnia,constipation, dry mouth
Medicine:	Orlistat
Effects:	Decreases fat absorption by inhibiting lipase in the intestine (not absorbed)

Proven efficacy, even long-term usage improves TC, LDL, TG, HbA1c, (glucose)

Side-effects: Oily spotting, flatulence, incontinence, worse after fat ingestion; can lead to less fat eaten Multi-vitamins with vitamins A, D, E, K recommended

5. SURGERY:

For high-risk patients who have failed non-surgical therapy

BMI 35 - 39.9 w/ RFs

BMI > 40

Produces longest weight loss maintenance of all treatment methods and significantly decreases mortality rate. Techniques used are vertical gastric banding, gastric bypass.

Summary of treatment based on BMI and risk

BMI 25 - 30, no RF: advise weight loss

BMI 27 - 29.9, > 2 RF: treat, +/- meds BMI 30 - 35: treat, +/- meds

BMI 35 - 39.9, no RF: treat, +/- meds

BMI 35 - 39.9, + RF: treat; +/- meds; consider surgery

BMI > 40: treat; +/- meds; consider surgery

SUMMARY OF THE LESSON

BMI > 30 defines obesity

Combined treatment with exercise, diet and behaviour modification is most effective

Set a reasonable goal of 5-10% weight loss

Start exercise slowly; emphasize benefits even if it doesn't result in weight loss

Follow-up frequently and monitor

Consider meds/surgery for high-risk patients

WHAT IS FIRST AID AND THE AIM OF FIRST AID

It is an immediate treatment given to the injured victim of an accident or sudden illness before the medical help is obtained. The aim of first aid is to preserve life, to promote recovery, to prevent worsening of the victim's condition and to arrange transportation to the hospital.

Scope of First Aid : The first aider should examine the victim to know the details of injuries and their nature.

Sign and Symptoms: The signs are what ever the first aider can find out for himself - bleeding, swelling any deformation of limbs etc. The symptoms, on the other hand, are what the victim tells the first aider of what he feels, like pain, shivering, faintness etc.

Role of First Aider : The best advice to first aider is:

(i) Reach the spot quickly as this could help save the life.

(ii) Be calm, methodical and prompt.

(iii) Look for the following:

(a) Is there failure of breathing (nose, stomach)

(b) Is there severe bleeding.

(c) Is the shock severe or light.

(d) Attend to these and then treat easily observable injuries.

(iv) Use the available first aid equipment.

(v) Clear the crowd around the victim gently. Do not allow people to crowd around the victim.

(vi) Note the weather, if it is raining, hot or a cold breeze isblowing, move the victim into a room.

(vii) Reassure the victim with soft words and encouraging talks. That will make the victim take things easy and lay quietly. This will help recovery.

(viii) Arrange for transportation to a hospital and at the same time intimate the relatives where the victim is being taken to.

Contents of First Aid box

The essential contents of first aid box are:

(i) Antiseptics (ii) Dressing Materials(iii) Articles (instruments) (iv) Others

The First aid box is maintained in the following ways:

(a) List of content should be enclosed

(b) Register for attendance of casualty.

(c) On the First Aid Box, a Red cross is placed on the white back ground which is easily visible.

Antiseptics used in the First aid box are:

1. Dettol in the ratio of 1: 20

2.Boric powder

3. Savlon in the ration of 1 : 20
4. Iodine
5. Benzene

Dressing materials are:

1. Gauze pieces
2.Cotton
3.Bandages (roller, trianguler, crêpé etc)
4.Adhesive plaster
5. Sterile pads and absorbent pads
6.Shell dressing

Articles used in the first aid box are:

1. Scissors
2.Forceps (artery, dissecting, skim, holding etc.)
3. Surgical blades

Other materials are :

1. Match box
2.Torch
3. Spirit

PREVENTION AND FIRST-AID FOR COMMON SPORTS INJURIES

The theory which leads sports injury is " Prevention is better than cure" and it is not whether you win or lose. There is a risk of injury just by participating . Sports injuries are not uncommon and can be either acute (sprains, fractures, tears, etc.) or chronic (tendinitis, overuse, etc.) Learn how to recognize and treat the most common sports injuries so they heal properly. Some can be treated at home, and some require a trip to the doctor. It's important to understand your options. Almost anyone who exercises on a regular basis will develop an ache, pain or sports injury at some time or another. The number and types of sports injuries are as varied as the individuals who play sports, but some injuries are more likely than others.

HOW DO SPORTS INJURIES OCCUR?

Injuries happen in three distinctive ways and they can be the result of:

(a) External Violence (b) Internal Violence (c) Over-use

(a) External Violence : Injuries that are the result of the body coming into contact with something external to the performer. This can be physical contact with another player or being hit by equipment or implements or coming into contact with the ground or other parts of the field of play.

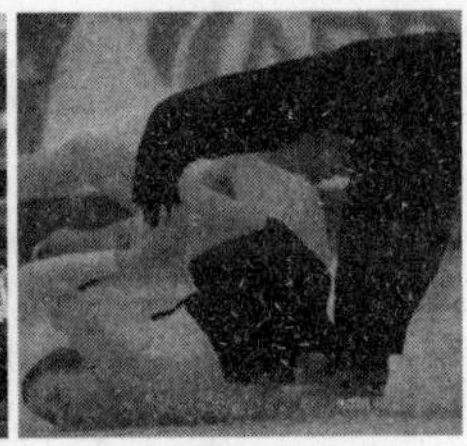

Eg: contact collusion, contact with ground/equipment/on players etc.

(b)Internal Violence: This is when a part of the performers body fails to cope with the stress placed upon it. Pulled Muscle, Torn Muscle, Ruptured Tendon, Pulled Ligaments, Cramp, Joint injuries,Impact injuries etc.

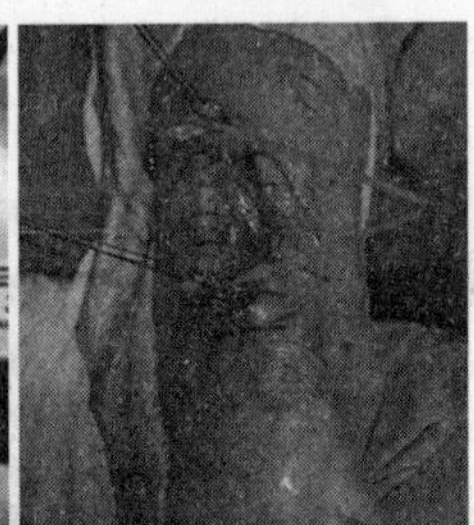

(c)Over Use Injuries : When one part of the body is used over and over again. This places a strain on the body part causing repetitive strain.

The following chart will give an idea how to prevent the sports injuries:

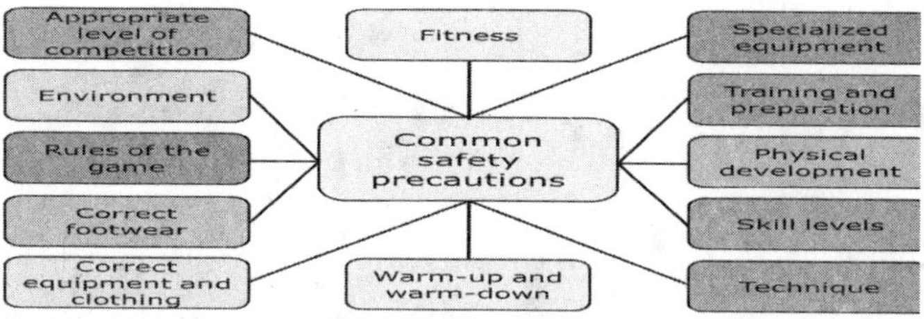

To guard against injury there should be three parts to an exercise session:

(1) The warm-up for activity: Preparing the body for work, a warm-up should precede any physical activity, whether training or competing and there are three phases of warm-up known as (i) Aerobic phase (ii) Stretch and flexibility phase (iii) Skills and intensive exercise.

(i) **Aerobic phase:** light aerobic work such as marching on the spot or jogging will start a session gradually.

(ii) **Stretch and flexibility phase:** muscles and joints are eased into positions appropriate to the activity.

(iii) **Skills and intensive exercise phase:** this phase contains slow stretching of muscles beyond their normal positions and held for short periods of time.

There are a number of reasons for warming-up prior to physical activity. The heart rate is gradually increased to nearer the working rate through pulse raising activities and body temperature is gradually increased to nearer the working rate.

It gradually stretches and moves the muscles and joints in ways that will be used in competition. It introduces skills to be used in competition. It increases the intensity of activities so that the body is prepared for competitive speed. Systematically working through the routine will prepare the performer's mind for the competition - this may give him a better start than the opposition. Allows players to work in small groups in the way they will in the game.

(b) **The main activity:** the activity, match or competition. This could be a training session, skills session or a competition, match or performance. Once the body is fit enough to complete the skills practised, the body can be pushed to the limit in competition without breaking down due to inadequate fitness levels.

(c) **The warm-down:** preparing the body to return to rest after the main activity. The body is given a chance to gradually return to its resting state. A gentle aerobic warm-down helps to do this. There are two phases to the warm-down (a) The gentle aerobic phase (b) The stretching phase. By completing a cool-down, the heartbeat reaches its resting rate sooner; this is called the recovery time. Therefore, the heart does not have to work too hard for longer than it needs to. The speed of the recovery rate after exercise is influenced by several factors: The older a person is, the slower the recovery rate will be. If the exercise is new, then the new stresses will be harder to recover from. The fitter a person is, the quicker the recovery rate. Women tend to recover more slowly than men.

By keeping the blood circulating it does not have the chance to 'pool' or collect in areas of the circulatory system; this prevents light-headedness. Gentle stretching stops the build-up of lactic acid in the muscles and so prevents immediate cramp and aching and soreness the following day. A controlled, restful warm-down can have a calming effect on a person after the excitement of a competitive match.

2. **Correct technique and safe practice:** Correct technique and safe practice are essential to all sports and activities. The coach is responsible for teaching players the correct skills and the laws of the game. Players need to learn the correct techniques in order to prevent risk of injury and achieve success. Training also improves body strength, helping it to deal with the stresses of an event, reduces fatigue, thereby helping prevent injury.
3. **Clothing and equipment:** In sporting activities where there is physical contact there is a danger of injury. This could be due to impact from other players, clothing, equipment or because excessive strain is put on the body. Players should make sure that their protective equipment is in good working order and allows for adequate movement. It should always be used during training and events. The size is correct and fit and not damaged. Clothing should be appropriate for the event such as in outdoor and adventurous activities. For example, when mountaineering, clothing needs to suit a wide spectrum of weather conditions and range from undergarments to outer layers. Boots should be comfortable, waterproof, sturdy and have a good grip.
4. **Rules and codes of conduct:** Each game will have its own set of rules or laws. These are designed to make the event safer and fairer for all involved. The governing body of the sport will create the rules, the coach teaches the players these rules, the playersthen adhere to these rules. The referee, umpire or judge then makes sure that everyone plays to these rules during the event. It is important that everyone involved with the event knows and understands the rules. There may be specific terminology used, procedures to follow or hand signals to perform.

   Codes of conduct, also known as etiquette, are the unwritten rules of behaviour a player stands by when competing.

For example, tennis players shake hands after a match and in cricket, a batsman might declare himself out and 'walk' as sometimes, only he will know if contact was made with the ball.

In terms of occurrence of injury the following can be factors: Clothing, Equipment, Footwear, Warm Up, Rules and Regulations, Protective Clothing, Warm Down.

Fitness Testing, Appropriate Level of Fitness, Knowledge of the Body, Facilities, Player Suitability, Training Methods, Age, Sex, Smoking, Drinking and Drugs.

CLASSIFICATION OF SPORTS INJURIES

There are two type of common sports injuries

(i) Acute Injuries: are the result of a sudden stress on the body. "injury characterized by rapid onset, resulting from a traumatic event" Acute injuries typically involve trauma followed by pain, swelling and loss of function. Critical force is the magnitude of a single force for which the anatomical structure of interest is damaged. For example, a dislocated shoulder caused by a tackle in rugby.

(ii) Chronic or Overuse Injuries: are injuries characterized by aslow, insidious onset, implying a gradual development of structural damage. They are caused by over training, insufficient recovery time, poor technique and badly designed footwear or equipment. Chronic injuries develop over time and are often associated with repetitive, cyclic activities, such as running. These injuries are commonly called "overuse injuries." Common sites include theAchilles tendon, patellar.

(a) Chronic Muscle Strain (b) Repetitive straining (c) Tendonitis (d) Irritated tendon, inflamed (e) Bursitis (f) Inflamed Bursa (g) With all chronic injuries it is important to discover what changed.

- **How to avoid acute injuries:** Consider the event itself by making sure you are playing at the right level for you. It can be dangerous to play against people who are bigger, stronger or more skilful. Know the rules of the sport and obey them as they were developed to protect you as well as test your skill. Pay attention to advice or warnings given by coaches, referees and other officials.
- **How to avoid chronic injuries:** It is necessary to develop the correct technique. For example, poor long distance running technique leads to back injuries. Choose your kit and equipment carefully, especially footwear. Allow enough time for full recovery between training sessions and/or events. Follow heavy training days with light days as your body adapts to training, it recovers. If you don't recover you'll gain no training adaptation.

TYPES OF WOUNDS

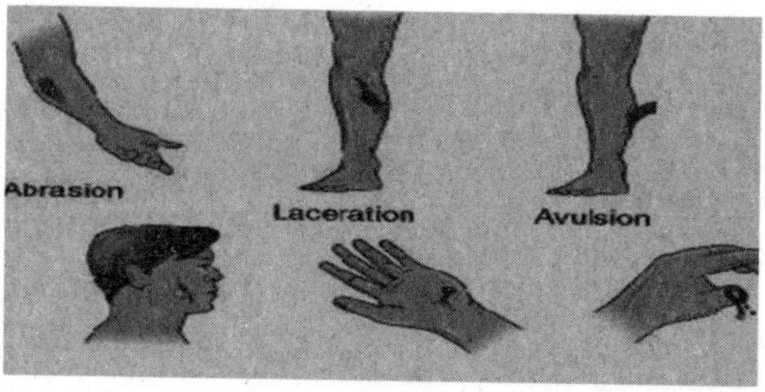

Head Injuries: You should place the person in the coma position making sure he can breathe easily - check nose and mouth for blockages - if he is not breathing you will need toperform CPR.

Bone and Joint Injuries: A fracture is a break or crack in a bone. In a simple or closed fracture the skin is not broken. In an open and compound fracture the skin is damaged too. Signs and Symptoms: The casualty may have heard or felt a snap and pain and tenderness around the injury. The casualty can't move the part normally and swelling and bruising occur. The limb may look deformed and twisted.

TYPES OF FRACTURE

There are several types of fracture. They differ from each other depending on the age of the bone and the type of impact, blow or pressure placed on it.

Greenstick: Pressure or impact buckles or bends a bone but only partially breaks it. This fracture is common in the developing bones of young children, whose bones are quite springy.

Closed fractures: These are more common and mean that the skin isn't broken. Open fractures involve the broken end of the bone coming through the skin .All fractures usually cause bruising and swelling because of associated damage to surrounding blood vessels. They are also very painful because nerves within the bone are damaged.

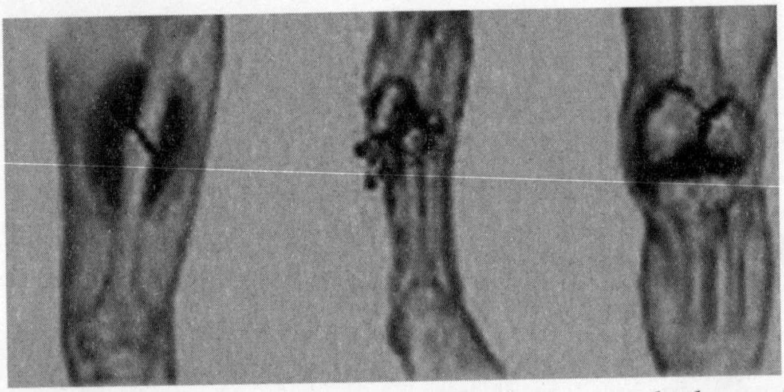

A stress fracture is a thin crack in the bone, which can be caused by overuse and continuous stress on the bone. These are common in the legs of runners and soldiers. Stress fractures are the only form of chronic bone injury, all other fractures are acute. Anysuspected fracture should be x-rayed.

Soft Tissue Injuries

These are basically anything that isn't bone! So injuries to muscles, ligaments, tendons, skin, cartilage etc. are all soft tissue injuries. Soft tissue injuries can be either chronic or acute. They can also be open or closed. Open injuries are when the skin is broken through as in cuts, grazes etc.

Closed injuries occur when the skin stays intact, and the injury is under the skin

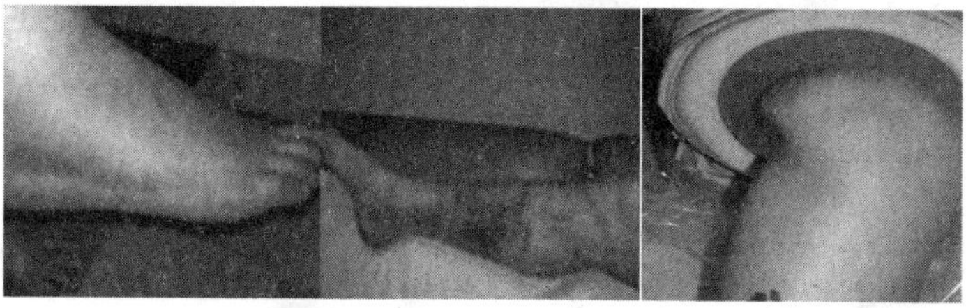

EXAMPLES:

Sprains - ligament damage. Ligaments attach bones to bones and keep a joint together. Sprains can occur as a result of a violent twisting or sideways movement to the joint (such as when you roll the ankle over)

Sprains - injuries to ligaments (three levels)
1st degree: Slightly torn ligament. No loss of function
2nd degree: Significantly torn ligament. Some loss of function
3rd degree: Completely torn ligament. Complete loss of function (1+joint surfaces displaced 3-5mm, 2+joint surfaces displaced 6-10mm and over, 1+ joint surfaces displaced over 10 mm)

First Aid and Treatment

1st degree level of sprain requires self-care through rehabilitation after the doctor's diagnosis Average healing time 2 to 6 weeks

2nd degree level of sprain requires physiotherapy after the doctor's diagnosis Average healing time 6 to 8 weeks

3rd degree level of sprain requires surgical repair and physical and physical therapy after the doctor's diagnosis.

Average healing time 8 to 10 weeks with the use of crutches, if necessary.

Strains - muscle damage. These are also known as pulled muscles and can vary in severity with some causing only minor damage and others tearing the whole muscle (a rupture). These are usually caused by overstretching. The hamstrings are the most common example.

Injuries to tendon, muscle or musculotendinous junction (Same 3 levels as above)

First Aid and Treatment

Grade 1 type: Mild strain - slightly pulled muscle with no tearing of muscle or tendon. No. loss of strength

- Ability to produce strong yet painful muscle contractions
- Requires self care through rehabilitation after doctor's diagnosis.
- Average healing time 2 to 10 days

Grade 2 type: Moderate strain-tearing of muscle tendon or at the bone attachment.

- Weak and painful attempts at muscular contraction.
- Requires physiotherapy after doctors diagnosis

Grade 3 type: Severe strain - rupture of muscle-tendon-bone attachment with separation.

- Extremely weak yet painless attempts at muscular contraction.
- Requires surgical repair and physiotherapy after doctor's diagnosis.
- Average healing time 6 to 10 weeks and possible use of crutches

Bruising - bleeding under the skin. This usually happens as a result of an impact such as being hit with a cricket ball. Contusion is another name for a bruise.

Dislocations - the displacement of contiguous surfaces of bones comprising a joint.

There are two types:
subluxation - partial displacement
Luxation - total displacement.

A bone is pulled away from the normal joint position. The most common example is the shoulder, where the humerus (arm bone) is pulled out of the socket. This can cause damage to the surrounding soft tissues and must be scanned with an MRI before being repositioned.

Cartilage tears - cartilage within the knee is most commonly injured. This happens through violent twisting or impacts which force the knee out of line.

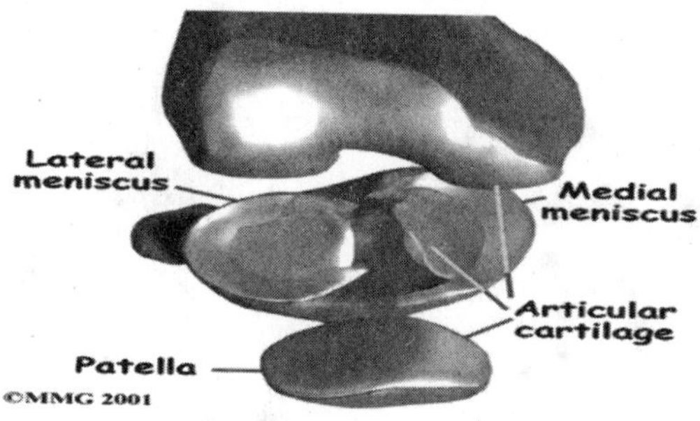

First Aid for Various Sports Injuries

Arm Slings: are used when both the elbow and arm and forearm need to be immobilised. They are used in case of injury to upper limbs and fore arm bones.

Triangular bandages: are triangular in shape. They are used to immobilise the limb, to support the limb, to keep the sling in position and to control the bleeding.

Small arm slings: are tied to a casualty to provide support to the arm including the elbow and to elevate the forearm giving comfort. The small arm sling provides support to the lower third of the forearm up to the base of the little finger.

Triangular Slings: are used to give comfort to the patient who is suffering from a collar bone fracture.

Collar and cuff slings: are extremely useful in cases where it is desirable to restrict the amount of movements of the elbow joint.
Stretcher Blanketing: will help to keep the casualty warm and will protect him against bumps and jolts. The face should be exposed in order to avoid suffocation and irritation.
Scalp bandages: are use in order to hold a light dressing on the scalp, though it cannot exert enough pressure to control the bleeding. It should be tied lightly otherwise a headache will result. The sustained part of the bandage is required to cross the ends at a fairly low level at the back of the head.
Fracture of the Clavicle: It may occur due to a fall forward on to the arm with the full weight of the body thrown on the arms

Symptoms of a fractured clavicle are pain, swelling, tenderness.

First Aid procedure - tie two narrow bandages around each shoulder. Put padding underneath the injured shoulder. Put a third bandage tied on the back between the two rings at the armpits. Tighten it to make the arm secure and comfortable. Then apply a triangular sling to support the weight.
Weight of the arm should be supported by an assistant whiletriangular sling is being applied.

Skull fracture: sign and symptoms of a skull injury are bleeding from the scalp, bleeding from the ear or nose, black eye and unequal dilation of pupil. Treatment -place the victim in a half sitting position, if he/she is conscious. If there is any discharge, incline the head toward the injured side, do not plug the ear if there is any bleeding. If unconscious but breathing, put him on a recovery position. If the victim is suffering from shock, treat him for shock.

Lower jaw fracture: signs and symptoms are difficulty in speaking and opening of the mouth. Blood stained spit.

Pain in jaw increased by speaking and swallowing. Swelling of face and lower jaw. Irregular teeth, crepitus sound on opening mouth. Treatment - maintain breathing ensuring the airway is clear, control bleeding and treat wounds. If the patient is conscious, sit him up with the head well forward to allow any secretions to drain away. Clear the mouth completely and tie the bandage.

Fracture of Ribs: Signs and symptoms are an increase in pain when the casualty takes short and shallow breaths. Crepitus sound may usually felt if a hand is placed on the ribs. If there is any open wound, apply a seal dressing. **Treatment** - if there are no complications (1) Two broad bandages should be applied around the chest (2) The centre of the first should be below the area of pain and the centre of the second above it. (3) The upper bandage should overlap the lower by half its width. (4) Instruct the casualty to breath out as much as he can and then tie the knot firmly so as to support the broken rib. (5)The knot should be tied nearer the front of the chest on the injured side. (6)Support the arm on the side of the injury in a sling.

Fracture of Elbow: (1) If the elbow can be bent, strap the arm to the chest, support the forearm in a triangular sling. (2) If the elbow cannot be bent, place the injured limb to one side of the trunk. Do not attempt to bend the elbow forcibly. (3) Place soft padding between the injured limb and the body. (4) Secure the injured limb to the body by three broad bandages around the wrist and thighs, the upper arm and trunk, and around the forearm and trunk.(5) Shift the casualty on a stretcher.

Nasal bone fracture: signs and symptoms are bleeding from the nose, blocking of the airway and difficulty in breathing. Treatment - (1) Stop the bleeding from the nose using a cold compress. (2) Clear the airway.

Fracture of Neck: signs and symptoms are severe pain in the back, loss of control over limbs, loss of sensation in the skin below the level of injury, irregularity may be felt over the spine. **Treatment** -do not move the casualty, loosen clothing at neck and fit a neck collar and maintain air way.

Fracture of Hand and Fingers: signs and symptoms are swelling, bruising at the site of injury. Treatment - control bleeding and treat any wounds, protect the injured hand by placing it in a fold at soft padding, gently support the affected limb in an elevation sling. For additional support, secure the limb to the chest by applying a broad bandage over the sling. Tie the knot in front of the injured side and shift him to the hospital.

Fracture of Thigh Bone (Femur): This is the longest bone of the body and it has rich blood supply. In this fracture a large volume of blood is lost in the tissues. This could result in severe shock.

Sign and symptoms - pain and swelling, visible deformity and shortening of the limb and signs of shock. Treatment - (1) treat the shock, immobilise the thigh by bandaging it to the second limb up to below knee with padding below the knees. If a splint is easily available use it. (2) Apply a well-padded splint between the legs from the crotch to the foot. (3) Tie the feet and ankles to the splint with a figure of 8 bandage. (4) A long well-padded splint from the axilla reaching up to foot should be applied. (5) Apply broad bandages at the following places: chest - below the armpit and pelvis at the level of hip joint. (6) Shift the casualty to hospital immediately

Fracture of Knee Caps: signs and symptoms are a loss of movement at the knee joint, severe pain in front of the knee, inability to bend the knee, tenderness, swelling and bruising at knee. Treatment - (1) Lay the casualty on his back with head and shoulders raised and supported by a rolled blanket. (2) Gently raise and support the injured limb on a splint, extending from thebuttocks to beyond the heel, the whole covered with adequate padding. (3) Apply extra padding under the knee just enough to fill the hallow behind the knee. Place adequate padding under the mattress in order to raise it of the splint. (4) Apply figure of 8 bandages around the thigh and splint, around the lower leg and splint and tie off on the outer side of the fractured limb.(5) Shift the casualty to hospital.

RICE TREATMENT: (RICE)Standard treatment for soft tissue injuries is

R- REST, I-ICE, C-COMPRESSION,
E- ELEVATION

R: Rest - means stop using the injured part, continued activity could cause further injury, delay healing, increase pain and stimulate bleeding. Use crutches to avoid bearing weight on injuries of the leg, knee, ankle and foot. Use splints for injuries of the arm, elbow, wrist, or hand.

I: Ice - hastens healing time by reducing the swelling around the injury.

- sudden cold contracts blood vessels.
- helps stop internal bleeding from injured capillaries and blood vessels.
- keep damp or dry cloth between skin and ice pack
- do not apply ice for longer than 15 to 20 minutes at a time.
- apply for 3 days after injury

If the symptoms persist

- apply every hour for 10 to 20 minutes
- apply ice after 3 days as long as pain or inflammation persists
- apply at least 3 times throughout the day for 15 to 20 minutes.

C: Compression - hastens healing time by reducing the swelling around the injury. It decreases seepage of fluids into injured area from adjacent tissue.

- use elastic bandage, compression sleeve, or cloth.
  - ∗ do not impair blood supply
  - ∗ excessively tight compression may cause more swelling
  - ∗ wrap over
  - ∗ loosen the bandage if it gets too tight.

E: Elevation - elevate the injured part above level of heart

- decreases swelling and pain
- use objects and pillows for props

Types of shock:

Primary shock - faintness which comes on straight after an emotional or traumatic event - passes quite quickly with reassurance and keeping warm.

True shock - far more serious. This comes about after a serious injury e.g. a bad cut or fracture. The person will be close to collapse, grey in colour and probably shaking. It is essential that he is treated in hospital. Call an ambulance immediately.

HEAT TREATMENT: May cause delay in healing if applied too soon after the injury.

wait at least 72 hours (3 days)

wait until swelling is gone

some experts recommend going back and forth between cold and heat treatment

HOT ICE THERAPY: Take a five litre bucket and put 2 litres normal water and 30 pieces of ice cubes in the bucket. Allow the temperature of the content to reach 34*F. If it has not reached 34*F put more ice cubes.

How to apply : take a 4 inch band aid (according to the size of injury) immerse the band aid inside the water and then apply to the injured part for 5,10,15,20 minutes according to the size of part and injury.

SAUNA BATH: It is a receiving method which provides for

muscular relaxation and recovery from fatigue. This method has been in use for a very long time in the field of sports especially forhigh performance.

Procedure	**Indications**
(i) Hot 2 minutes (dry heat)	(i) Temporary Weight loss
(ii) Cold 2 minutes bath	(ii) Muscular relaxation
(iii) Hot 3 minutes (dry heat)	(iii) releases toxins from body
(iv) Cold 3 minutes bath	(iv) Recovery from fatigue
(v) Hot 2 minutes (dry heat)	(v) Normal bath

Contraindications are heart patients, infectious diseases, High BP and pregnancy. They are recommended not to undergo this treatment. The post proceedings are lay down on the bed for 30 minutes, after that take plenty of water/ fruit juices. No alcohol/smoking for two and half hour after receiving it.

STEAM BATH: It is a receiving method for muscular relaxation, fatigue and weight loss by means of moist heat taken continuously for 7 to 15 minutes though the temperature may vary from person to person.

CONTRAST BATH: Take one bucket warm water/hot water (60 to 70 degrees Celsius) and one bucket of ice water (34*F). First cold water for 3 minutes and then 1 minute hot water. Next time 3 minutes cold and 2 minutes hot water. Then 2 minutes cold water and 3 minutes hot water followed by 1 minute cold water and 3 minutes hot water. Likewise the time for hot water should be increased and cold water time should be decreased. Minimum twice a day, a total of at least 10 minutes each time.

GENERAL RULES TO FOLLOW

Do not move the person unless you are sure of what the injury is. If he is unconscious, or has been, you must phone an ambulance as he must be checked out.

Look at the damaged area and see if there are any signs of injury -if it is obvious, cuts or wounds then ask if he can move the area of injury and stop the bleeding- by pressure with a clean cloth or bandage.

If there is no cut, talk to the person - ask if it hurts, can he move it. Then look for swellings, misshapen areas or tenderness. If he feels able to stand and move on his own then he should decide.

If he are able to continue - any doubts at all, stop. Continuing to play can really aggravate what may have been a non-serious injury.

If you have problems going through these stages then you must get expert help straight away. There is a big difference between first aid and medical treatment.

Key Terms:

Stress fractures - a break in the bone caused by repeated application of a heavy load or constant pounding on a surface, such as running

Tennis Elbow - a painful injury or inflammation of the tendon attached to the elbow joint

Dilated - enlarged, expanded or widened.

Sprains - the overstretching or tearing of ligaments at a joint

Strains - the overstretching of a muscle, rather than a joint.

MOST COMMON SPORTS INJURIES AND THEIR FIRST AID

1. OPEN WOUND

- Stop Bleeding
- Direct Pressure with gauze (if available)
- Stack gauze, do not remove it.
- Pressure points in severe cases (arteries)
- Clean with soap and water, irrigate with water, 5 min if possible
- Ointment (Neosporin, triple antibiotic, etc.)

- Cover with Band-Aid or other non-stick product.
- Stitches if necessary when the wound is ½ inch long or skin does not naturally come together.

2. ANKLE SPRAIN

It occurs when the foot turn inward and this turning stretches or tears the relatively weak ligaments on the outside of the ankle. It is important to exercise to prevent loss of flexibility and strength and re-injury. A high ankle sprain is slower to heal and should be seen by a doctor to make sure the bones in the lower leg did nor separate. One way to recognise a high ankle sprain is that this sprain usually causes tenderness above the ankle.

3. GROIN PULL

Pushing off in a side to side motion causes strain of the inner thigh muscle or groin. Compression, ice and rest will heal most groin injuries. Returning to full activity too quickly can aggravate a groin pull or turn into a long term problem. Any groin pull that has significant swelling should be seen to early by a doctor.

4. HAMSTRING STRAIN

Three muscles in the back of the thigh form the hamstring. The hamstring can be over stretched by movement such as hurdling or kicking the leg out sharply when running . Hamstring injuries are slow to heal because of the constant stress applied to the injured tissues from walking. Complete healing can take place over 6 to 12 months. Recurrence of the injury is common as it is hard to be inactive for such a long period. RICE followed by contrast treatment are good treatments for recovery.

5. SHIN SPLINT

Pain down the front of the lower legs are commonly called shin splints. They are most often brought about by running, especially when starting a more strenuous training program like long runs on paved roads. It also due to tight posthumous muscle imbalance, improper shoes and over training Rest, ice and over the counter pain medicine are the mainstays of treatment. This is commonly a stress fracture but you should see a doctor as it could be a small break in the shin bone.

Stress fractures require prolonged rest, usually a month or more, toheal. Another remedy to overcome this is training slightlymaintaining fitness, swimming, etc.

6. KNEE INJURY (ACL)

The anterior cruciate ligament (ACL) holds the leg bone to the knee. Sudden cuts or stops or getting hit from the side can strain or tear the ACL. A complete tear can make the dreaded "pop" sound. You must see a doctor if you suspect an injury of the ACL. It is one of the most common and severe sports injuries. A completely torn ACL requires surgery in individuals who wish to remain physically active.

7. KNEE INURY (Patello Femoral Syndrome)

It is the result of repeated movement of your kneecap (patella) against your thigh bone (femur), which can damage the tissue under the knee cap. Patience is the key to treatment. Knee pain can take up 6 weeks to clear up. It is important to continue low impact exercises during this time. Working out the quadriceps can also relieve pain.

8. TENNIS ELBOW

It is due to repetitive use of the elbow -playing tennis or golf regularly can irritate or make tiny tears in the elbow's tendon. Epicondylitis or tennis elbow, is most common in 30 - 60 years olds and usually involves the outside of the elbow. Rest and stopping the swinging activity will improve the condition and decrease the pain.

9. CRAMPS

They are due to a deficiency of vitamin E. Stretching the affected muscle, drinking plenty of water with salt content will clear it.

10. FATIGUE

Failure to sustain expected or required muscular force, because of exhaustion after normal activities. Steps to be taken into consideration for recovery of muscular injuries

T - Type : (a) Stretching (b) Isometric strength (c) Isotonic strength (d) Functional exercises

I - Intensity

D - Duration F - Frequency P – Progression

There are three types of common muscular injuries:

Contusion

Strain

Laceration/Tear-off

How injury occurs:

Inadequate warm-up

Tightness

Muscular imbalance

Fatigue

NUTRITION COMPONENTS, BALANCED DIET AND DIET FOR ATHLETES

Definition of nutrition

A function of living plants and animals, consisting of the taking in and metabolism of food material whereby tissue is built up and energy liberated. It is the study of the food and liquid requirements of human beings or animals for normal physiologic function, including energy needs, maintenance, growth, activity, reproduction, and lactation.

The food we eat determines the way we look and, to some

extent, the way we feel, think, and behave. Nutrition enrichment isthe composition of food and the importance of different articles in it. This includes vegetable sources (food stuffs available in India)

COMPOSITION OF FOOD:

Food is composed of the same chemicals that make up our bodies (water, salts, proteins, and so on). When we talk about diet, foods are classified according to the kinds of nutrients they provide. These nutrients (substances which are necessary for the body's growth and functioning) are proteins, carbohydrates, fats, minerals, and vitamins.

(1) PROTEINS: These are the basic substances of our bodies -the stuff out of which each cell is built. Proteins also provide energy. Protein is made up of carbon, hydrogen, oxygen and nitrogen. It is found in all cells.

Protein plays a unique role in the growth and repair of body tissue, and speeds up the rate of chemical reactions in the body.

All proteins are made up of amino acids - 11 of them can be produced by the body and 9 others must be supplied by food. The 9 that cannot be produced by the body are called essential amino acids.

There are two type of protein- (i) Complete protein: A protein that contains all 9 essential amino acids. (ii) Incomplete protein: A protein that lacks one or more of the essential amino acids. E.g. milk, nut, egg, soybean, pulses, dried peas, fish etc.

Deficiency of protein is especially harmful in childhood. It can lead to impairment of physical and mental growth. Children with deficiency are more likely to get frequent infections. In adults, though growth is complete, protein deficiency leads to weakness, inability to do hard work, frequent infections, and delayed wound healing.

(2)FATS: Fats are very concentrated sources of energy. They give twice as much energy as either proteins or carbohydrates. Those fats which exist in nature in the solid state are called fats. Those which are liquid by nature are called oils. Sources for fat are vegetable which include various edible oils (groundnut, gingerly, rape seed, coconut); and animal which include ghee, red meat, etc. There are two types of fats, (1) Saturated: Usually solid at room temperature and can be found in most animal fats. They contain single bonds between carbon atoms and the maximum number of bonds of hydrogen atoms.

Unsaturated: Liquid at room temperature and contain fewer bonds of hydrogen. These are generally found in plants. Some vegetable oils are hydrogenated and they are treated with particular temperature and pressure in the presence of a chemical. After this process they can be kept even in hot climates. In India, a popular example is 'vanaspati' (dalda). During the process, the vegetable oils lose certain essential components which promote growth and keep the skin healthy.

Why we need fat in our food: Fats store energy in a form that can be used when the body needs it. (a) They protect our organs. (b) They insulate our body from the cold. (c) They transport certain vitamins throughout the body. (d) They are an important ingredient of several hormones.

Know cholesterol : Cholesterol is a fat like substance that is part of all animal cells and is needed for the production of some hormones and fat digestion. There are two types of cholesterol (1) HDL (high-density lipoproteins) are compounds that remove cholesterol from the blood and transport it back to the liver. (2) LDL (low-density lipoproteins) are compounds that carry cholesterol to the cells for cell processing.

(3) CARBOHYDRATES: Carbohydrates are more commonly known as starches and sugars. They provide heat and energy. Digestive juices convert these foods into glucose, which is the form of sugar found in the blood. Glucose is the fuel for the activity of all the cells.

There are two types of carbohydrates.

(1) **Complex** - are low in fat and rich in vitamins, minerals and fibre. These include: pasta, rice and whole grains. These are a longer lasting energy source.

(2) **Simple** - are low in fat, missing some essential vitamins and mineral and are a short term energy source.

Dietary fibre: A complex carbohydrate that does not provide energy. It is commonly called roughage. It helps to move undigested food through the digestive tract preventing constipation and reducing the risk of certain diseases. Carbohydrates also provide the bulk of fibre or roughage. This is in the form of cellulose, which is the fibrous material present in many fruit and vegetables. Sources are cereals, starchy vegetables such as potatoes, corn, rice bran, whole grains, greens and veggies.

(4) VITAMINS: Vitamins are complex chemical substances required by the body in very small amounts. There are about a dozen vitamins which are essential for good health. Vitamins are not produced in the body. However, a well-balanced diet supplies all the vitamins, their actions, symptoms of deficiency, and sources have been given below.

SOME VITAMINS IN RELATIONS TO HUMAN LIFE

Vitamins	Symptoms of deficiency	Action in body	Good Sourcess
A	Night Blindness	Normal vision Normal growth	Carrot Mango Papaya
B1	Weakness Altered nerves function	Normal nerves function	Whole cereals sprouts

B2	Pellagra(Dermatitis, Diarrhoea, Dementia)	Normal metabolism of protein, fats& carbohydrates	Whole cereals Sprouts
B3	Skin disease Altered nerves functions	Normal growth	Whole cereals Sprouts
Folic Acid	Anaemia	Normal production of red cells	Green leaf Vegitables
Ascorbic acid/C	Scurvy fatigue, Haemorrhage Abnormalities of bones	Wound healing Increased resistance to infections	Fresh Fruits (orange, lemons, amala, gooseberry)
D	Rickets- Defective bones and muscles	Normal growth of bones and teeth. Normal muscle tone	Milk and milk products

Vitamins are organic substances that assist in the chemical reactions that occur in the body. Fat soluble vitamins are

A: maintains healthy eyes, skin, bones, teeth and keeps the lining of digestive track resistant to infections.

D: promotes normal growth.

E: prevents the destruction of red blood cells.

K: assists with blood clotting. Water soluble vitamins are:

B1: (Thiamine) assists with conversion of carbohydrates to energy.

B2: (Riboflavin) assists with nerve cell function.

B3: (Niacin) maintenance of normal metabolism.

B12: necessary for formation of red blood cells and normal cell function.

B6: (Pyridoxine) necessary for normal carbohydrate, fat and protein metabolism.

FOLACIN: necessary for the production of genetic materials.

BIOTIN: necessary for metabolism of carbs. and other B vitamins.

PANTOTHENIC ACID: used to produce some hormones

and assist with the release of energy.

C: (Ascorbic Acid) needed for normal development of connective tissue.

5.MINERALS: Minerals required by the body include calcium, iron, and iodine (though iodine is usually described as a 'trace element'). Minerals are Inorganic substances that are generally absorbed to form structural components of the body.

Calcium: is necessary for the maintenance of the teeth and bones, for clotting of blood, and for muscular contraction. Sources: milk and milk products, dried fruit (specially dates), fresh fruit ('sitaphal' or custard apple), and certain cereals, such as ragi.

Iron: is a component of haemoglobin (the red colouring substance in the blood), and of myoglobin (the red colouring substance in the muscles). It is concerned with oxygen transport and cellular respiration. Deficiency of iron affects the formation of haemoglobin, which is present in lower than normal amounts. This is called anaemia. Sources: dried fruits, nuts, jaggery, dried peas and beans, and green leafy vegetables.

Iodine: Is important as it is used by the thyroid gland to synthesize the hormones, thyroxine and triodothyronine. These two hormones influence the body growth and metabolism.

Deficiency of iodine leads to low levels of the thyroid hormone in the blood. Hence the feedback or check on the anterior pituitary and hypothalamus is removed. As a result, the hypothalamus releases the releasing hormone (RH), which brings about release of the stimulating hormones (SH) of the anterior pituitary. The SH stimulate the thyroid gland, which increases in size - this is called goitre. Though enlarged, it is unable to produce the hormones, till iodine is provided. Sources: sea salt, sea food, cereals, and nowadays 'iodized salt'.

CHLORINE: maintenance of water balance.
COPPER: involved in skin colour.
MAGNESIUM: needed for chemical reactions. MANGANESE: normal function of nerve cells. PHOSOHORUS: plays a role in metabolism.
POTASSIUM: nerve and muscle function.
SODIUM: water balance and nerve conduction.
SULFUR: found in amino acids.
ZINC: needed for digestion, respiration, healing and metabolism. Nutrition deficiencies:
Night blindness and impaired growth can result from a lack of vitamin A.
Rickets and/or inadequate growth of bones and teeth come from a lack of vitamin D.
Lack of vitamin E can result in anaemia.
Lack of vitamin K can cause slow blood clotting.
Deficiency in B1 can result in muscle weakness and heart problems.
Skin sores can be caused by the lack of vitamin B2.
Lack of B3 is a contributing factor of depression.
Skin disorders and hair loss can be caused by a lack of BIOTIN.

6. WATER: Water is an essential component in your diet and about 2/3 of your body weight is water. About 65 to 70% of men's body weight is water and About 55 to 65% of women's body weight is water. All body functions are a result of chemical reactions and most need water to occur. It helps maintain acidity at the proper

level so the chemical reactions can occur. Water helps transport gases, nutrients and waste throughout the body. Water regulates body temperature and produces the chemical reaction that helps drive your body processes.

Dehydration : A state in which the body has lost more water than has been taken in. Dehydration can occur as a result of heavy physical activity or an illness that includes vomiting, diarrhoea, fever or a situation that causes one to sweat profusely. This can happen if there is an insufficient intake of water.

BALANCED DIET: These are guidelines set so that you may select foods that provide you with a nutritionally balanced diet.

Teens / Adults
Males & Females

- **Age**
- **Weight**
- **Height**
- **Activity level**
- **Expectation**
- **Choices**

Example

- **Some guidelines today, suggest this is the proper balance a teenager needs in there diet.**

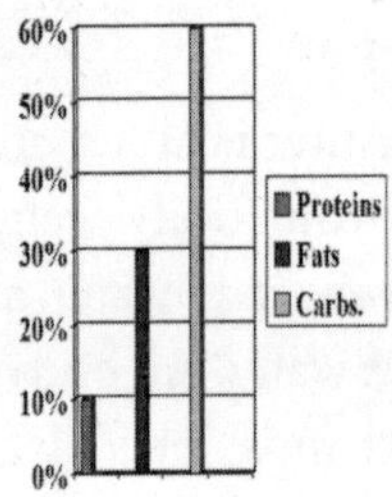

How much you should take:

Carbohydrates = 6 to 11 servings, Vegetables = 3 to 5 servings, Fruits = 2 to 4 servings

Dairy = 2 to 3 servings, Protein = 2 to 3 servings, Fats = not a food group, use sparingly.

What you need to consume each day depends on Age,

Gender, Activity, Expectation, Height, Weight, Choices.

The teens (both boys and girls) experience increased demands for energy, protein, vitamins, and minerals to deal with mental and physical changes. Protein for muscle growth, calcium and iron for developmental changes. Vegetarians choose not to eat meat products and some avoid dairy products as well. Since not all essential nutrients can be found in plants (B12), they must eat a very wide variety of veggies and take a supplement to be sure they are receiving the nutrients they need to maintain a healthy life. Elderly people's nutritional needs a similar to those of the general population. As you age you should continue to eat a variety of foods to reduce the likelihood of missing important nutrients

Balanced diet for Athletes:

They have specific nutritional needs for their training and performance requirements. The amount of calories consumed depends of the type of activity. One thing is for sure, they MUST drink water before, during and after workouts. Athletes need to consume adequate energy during periods of high-intensity and/or long-duration training to maintain body weight and health and maximize training effects.

Low energy intakes can result in: loss of muscle mass;

menstrual dysfunction;

loss of or failure to gain bone density;

an increased risk of fatigue, injury, and illness; and a prolonged recovery process.

Body weight and composition should not be used as the sole criterion for participation in sports; daily weigh-ins for this purpose are discouraged. Optimal body fat levels depend on the sex, age, and heredity of the athlete and may be sport-specific. Body fat assessment techniques have inherent variability and limitations.

Carbohydrate recommendations for athletes range from 6 to 10 gms. to 1 kg body weight.

COMPLEX CARBOHYDRATES

Carbohydrates maintain blood glucose levels during exercise and replace muscle glycogen. The amount required depends on the athlete's total daily energy expenditure, type of sport, sex, and environmental conditions.

Protein recommendations for endurance and strength-trained athletes range from 1.2 to 1.7 gms. to 1 kg body weight. These recommended protein intakes can generally be met through diet alone, without the use of protein or amino acid supplements.

The current recommended dietary allowance (RDA) is 0.8 gms. to 1kg body weight and the acceptable macronutrient distribution range (AMDR) for protein intake for adults older than 18 yr is 10%-35% of total calories. Energy intake sufficient to maintain bodyweight is necessary for optimal protein use and performance.

Fat intake should range from 20% to 35% of total energy intake. Consuming < 20% of energy from fat does not benefit performance. Fat, which is a source of energy, fat-soluble vitamins, and essential fatty acids, is important in the diets of athletes. High-fat diets are not recommended for athletes.

Athletes who restrict energy intake or use severe weight-loss practices, eliminate one or more food groups from their diet, or consume high or low carbohydrate diets of low micronutrient density are at greatest risk of micronutrient deficiencies. Athletes should consume diets that provide at least the recommended dietary allowance (RDA) for all micronutrients.

Water: The goal of drinking is to prevent dehydration from occurring during exercise and individuals should not drink in excess of their sweating rate. After exercise, approximately 16-24 oz (450-675 ml) of fluid for every pound (0.5 kg) of body weight lost during exercise. Before exercise, a meal or snack should provide sufficient fluid to maintain hydration, be relatively low in fat and fibre to facilitate gastric emptying and minimize gastrointestinal distress, be relatively high in carbohydrates to maximize maintenance of blood glucose, be moderate in protein, be composed of familiar foods, and be well tolerated by the athlete. During exercise, primary goals for nutrient consumption are to replace fluid losses and provide carbohydrates (approximately 30-60 gms. h-1) for maintenance of blood glucose levels.

During exercise: These nutrition guidelines are especially important for endurance events lasting longer than an hour when the athlete has not consumed adequate food or fluid before exercise or when the athlete is exercising in an extreme environment (heat, cold, or high altitude).

Post exercise: After exercise, dietary goals are to provide adequate fluids, electrolytes, energy, and carbohydrates to replace muscleglycogen and ensure rapid recovery.

RECOVERY:

A carbohydrate intake of approximately 1.0-1.5 gms to 1 kg body weight (0.5-0.7 gms. lb-1) during the first 30 min and again every 2 hours for 4-6 hours will be adequate to replace glycogen stores. Protein consumed after exercise will provide amino acids for building and repair of muscle tissue. In general, no vitamin and mineral supplements are required if an athlete is consuming adequate energy from a variety of foods to maintain body weight. A multivitamin/mineral supplement may be appropriate if an athlete is dieting, habitually eliminating foods or food groups, is ill or recovering from injury, or has a specific micronutrient deficiency.

Single nutrient supplements may be appropriate for a specific medical or nutritional reason (e.g., iron supplements to correct iron deficiency anaemia).

MEANING AND DEFINITION OF DOPING, ERGOGENIC AIDS

Doping is the use of methods or taking substances (usually various forms of medicaments) which in an artificial way will increase physical performance capacity. Doping is forbidden on medical as well as sports ethical grounds. The word 'dope' originated from a primitive South African alcoholic drink that was used as a stimulant in ceremonial dances. In today's sporting context, doping refers to the use of performance enhancing chemicals of banned substances or methods that may enhance the performance of an athlete.

List of doping classes and methods:

1.Prohibited Classes Of Substances

A.Stimulants

B.Narcotics

C.Anabolic Agents

D.Diuretics

E.Peptide and glycoprotein hormones

2. Prohibited Methods

A. Blood doping

B. Pharmacological, chemical and physical manipulation

3. Classes Of Drugs Subject To Restriction.

A. Alcohol
B. Marijuana
C. Local Anaesthetics
D. Corticosteroids
E. Beta-Blockers

(A) Stimulants: Examples: Amphetamines, Ephedrine, Cocaine, Caffeine etc. positive effects are its produce alertness, Wakefulness may increase hostitlity, Reduce fatigue, Less sensitivity to pain, Increase in ability to concentrate, Increase endurance and speed. Commonly used by Athletics, Football, Cycling, Swimming, Wrestling, Boxing players.

(B) Narcotics: Examples: Pethidine, Morphine, Heroine etc. The positive effect is that they are powerful pain killers. Side effects are:

1. Dose related respiratory depression
2. Physical and psychological dependence
3. Increase of the pain threshold resulting in the failure to recognize injury leading to more serious injury
4. Impaired judgement
5. Addiction
6. Loss of muscular co-ordination
7. Nausea, Vomiting, Dizziness, Mental clouding

(c) Anabolic Agents/Steroids: These are synthetic derivatives of the male hormone testosterone, they produce both androgenic and anabolic effects. Examples: stanozolol, Methyl test, Testosterone, Dianabol, Nandrolone etc.

Types Of Anabolic Steroids:

Oral: Dianabole, Stromba, Nuvir, Oraboline etc.

Water Soluble Inj: Testosterone

Fast Soluble Inj: Methandiol, Dromestelone, Nandrolone,

Testosterone propionate.

Advantages are (1) Increase in muscle development (2) Increase in muscular strength (3) Increase in aggressiveness (4) Helps totrain harder and for longer periods

Commonly used by: Wrestlers, Weightlifters, Boxers, Body builders, Throwers, Power lifters.

Side effects:

1. **In females**: (i) More common - Acne and Oily Skin, Enlarged Clitoris, Hoarseness or Deepening of Voice.(ii) Irreversible - Irregular Menstrual Periods, Unnatural Hair Growth, Unusual Hair Loss (iii) Less Common - Mental Depression, Unusual Tiredness, Infertility.
2. **In pre-pubertal males** (i) More Common - Acne, Enlarged Penis, Increased Frequency of Erection, Unnatural Hair Growth (ii) Less Common - Unexplained Darkening Of Skin
3. **In Males Only:** (i) Acne, Increase in Aggressiveness and Sex Vigour, Reduction in Testicular Size and Sperm Production, Breast Enlargement, Premature Baldness, Kidney Dysfunction, Cholesterol.

Synthesis of testosterone: MEN - Testes and Adrenal Cortex

WOMEN- Ovaries and Adrenal Cortex

Mechanism of action: An increase in protein synthesis, Inhibition of catabolic effects of Glucocorticoids, effects on CNS and neuromuscular junction, the Placebo effect.

Mechanism of action of steroid are: (i) Increase in protein synthesis in the muscle (ii) Blocks the catabolic (muscle destroying) effect of cortisone secreted by the adrenal glands in reaction to exercise and stress (iii) converts negative Nitrogen balance to positive balance by improving utilisation of ingested protein (iv) steroid induced enhancement of aggressive behaviour that promotes a greater quantity and quality of weight training.

Why do athletes take steroids? Because the effect increases muscle strength and allows them to train harder and longer and to increase their competitiveness.

(D) **Diuretics:** examples are Lasix, Dyide, Spironoactone etc. They are used to reduce body weight quickly in sports , reduce concentration of drugs in urine and commonly used by Athletes, Boxers, Judo, Power lifters, Weight lifters, Wrestlers, Weight Category Sports people. Side effects are: dehydration and electrolyte imbalance, decrease VO2 Max, workload in maximal exercise and blood lactate level (Hypovolemia), muscular cramps, orthostatic hypotension, Hypokalemia if severe life threatening. "Elimination time 24-72 hrs"

(E) **Peptide and Glycoprotein Hormones:** HCG (Human Chorionic Gonadotrophine) - Administrated to males lead to increased rate of Endogenous Androgenic steroids and is equivalent to exogenous administration of testosterone.

Growth hormones : Misuse is unethical and dangerous because of various adverse effects. Allergic reactions, Diabetogenic effects and acromegaly when applied in high doses

Erythropoietin: Glycoprotein produced in the kidney which stimulates the production of RBC.

Prohibited Methods (A) Blood doping is the administration of blood or related red blood products obtained from the same or from a different individual to an athlete in an attempt to gain unfair advantage in competition by increasing the blood's oxygen carrying capacity.

RISK: (i) Alergicration (ii)Mismatched blood can be fatal (iii) Viral hepatitis (iv) Shock (v) Overloading of circulation and metabolic shock (vi) Kidney diseases.

Classes Of Drugs Subject To Restriction

(I) Beta Blockers: examples are: Atenolol, Etacard, Catenol, Atenova, Inderal, Sotalol, Betaloc etc. Advantages of use -reduction of the heart rate and cardiac output will lead to better performance in certain sports like rifle shooting. They steady the trigger finger and nerves, remove anxiety. But they also have side effects like a tendency to induce sedation, sleep disturbances, cold hands and cardiac arrest. Beta Blockers are tested only in Archery, Shooting, Sailing, Gymnastics, Fencing, Equestrians, Diving, Ski-jumping, and Golf.

(II) Alcohol: Prohibited in :Aeronautic (0.20 g/L), Power boating (0.30 g/L), Archery, Automobile, Boules, Motorcycling, Karate, Modern Pentathlon including Shooting (all 0.10 g/L). Breath or blood alcohol levels may be determined at the request of a federation. Side effects - CNS depressant. Results in impairment of judgement, reflexes and muscular coordination.

(III)Corticosteroids: to reduce inflammation. Causes mood changes including, Euphoria, Osteoporosis, softening of connective tissue and weakening of an injured area in muscles, joints, tendons or ligaments. Prohibited orally, intravenous, intramuscularly, rectally. Use requires T.U.E. Other routes of administration

Permitted: Topical preparations when used for dermatological, auricular, nasal, ophthalmological, gingival and perianal disorders.

No TUE/ATUE required.

(iv) Marijuana: Cannabis, Hashish Results in - impairment of Balance and Co-ordination, Drowsiness, Loss of Concentration.

Doping is cheating: Firstly cheating the opposition, Secondly cheating oneself, Thirdly cheating the public. The aim of anti-doping is to protect the athlete's health, defend principles of medical and sports ethics and uphold equal chance for one and all.

Sanctions against doping are : First offence any category a 2 year ban. The second offence gets one a life ban

ERGOGENIC AIDS:

Athletes should be counselled regarding the appropriate use ofergogenic aids. Such products should only be used after careful evaluation for safety, efficacy, potency, and legality. Ergogenic aid is defined as any substance or treatment that either directly improves physiological variables associated with exercise performance or removes subjective restraints that may limit physiologic capacity.

Types: (i) Psychological (ii) Mechanical (iii) Pharmacological (iv) Physiological (v)Nutritional

(i) Psychological ergogenic aids are (a) Hypnosis (b) Music (c) Performance Enhancement Techniques (PST) (d) "Placebo Effect" / Superstitions

(ii) Mechanical aids are clothing, equipment, heat and cold application, improved body mechanics, environment (playing conditions and surface).

(iii) Pharmacological aids are over the counter drugs like Caffeine, Nicotine, Amphetamines, Melatonin....etc; "Recreational" Drugs are Alcohol, Marijuana, Cocaine.......etc; Prescription Drugs are Anabolic Steroids, Benzodiazepines, Beta-Adrenergic Agents...... etc;

(iv) Physiological Agents are Bicarbonate Loading, Blood Doping, Erythropoietin (EPO) Altitude Training, Lycerol, Phosphate Loading etc.

(v) Nutritional Agents / Supplements are Amino Acid Supplementation, Bee Pollen Carbohydrate Loading, Carnitine, Coenzyme Q-10,Creatine Phosphate, Water or Special Beverages.

Chapter III

DEVELOPMENT OF FITNESS

BENEFITS OF PHYSICAL FITNESS AND EXERCISE

A formidable challenge facing many personal fitness trainers (PFTs) and other health and fitness professionals is finding new ways of motivating people to improve their well-being through consistent participation in physical activity and exercise. Daily exercise will enhance one's mental well-being and promote healthy musculoskeletal functions throughout life and habitual physical fitness regime is an attainable goal on the path to a healthier life. There is a growing understanding of how certain levels of physical activity may positively affect cardiovascular, musculoskeletal, respiratory and endocrine function, as well as mental health. The following lines will sum up the evidence on 25 significant benefits linking physical activity to health enhancement. Some of the benefits have been grouped together because of their physiological or metabolic associations.

1 **Cardiovascular Disease:** Meaningful cardiovascular health benefits may be attained with long-term participation in cardiovascular exercise.

2 **Diabetes 3. Insulin Sensitivity 4. Glucose Metabolism:** Regular aerobic exercise meaningfully increases insulin sensitivity and glucose metabolism, which means the body's cells can transport glucose into the cells of the liver, muscle and adipose tissue more efficiently. Elevated insulin and blood glucose levels are characteristic features involved in the development of non-insulin-dependent diabetes mellitus. When the insulin function starts breaking down, the body's blood sugar levels rise, leading eventually to the onset of "prediabetes" and then type 2 diabetes. Diabetes incidence is growing among youth and adults, largely as a result of obesity and inactivity.

3 **Hypertension:** moderate-intensity aerobic exercise (40%-50% of VO2max), performed 3-5 times per week for 30-60 minutes per session, appears to be effective inreducing blood pressure. Although routine aerobic exercise usually will not affect the blood pressure of normotensive individuals, habitual aerobic exercise may be protective against the increase in blood pressure commonly seen with increasing age. During resistance exercises, systolic and diastolic blood pressures may show steep increases, which indicate that caution should be observed with persons with known CVD or CVD risk factors. These increases in blood pressure are dependent on the intensity of the contraction, the length of time the contraction is held and the amount of muscle mass involved in the contraction. More dynamic forms of resistance training, such as circuit training, that involve moderate resistance loads and high repetitions with short

rests are safe and associated with reductions in blood pressure.

4 **Blood Triglycerides 7. Cholesterol 8.LDL Cholesterol:** 15-20 miles per week of jogging or brisk walking, which is equivalent to 1,200-2,200 kilocalories of energy expenditure, may decrease blood triglycerides by 5-38 milligrams per decilitre (mg/dl). It is established that a sedentary lifestyle contributes significantly to the development of CHD and to unfavourable elevation of blood fats and cholesterol levels; physical activity plays an important role in decreasing these health risks. That same threshold of exercise (15-20 miles per week of jogging or brisk walking) has been shown to elevate HDL-C (a positive alteration) by 2-8 mg/dl.

Exercise training studies rarely show a decrease in total cholesterol or LDL-C (the bad cholesterol), unless there is a loss of body weight or a decrease in dietary fat (or both). The serum level of LDL-C has been shown to be significantly reduced among women (a decrease of 14.5±-22.2 mg/dl) and men (a decrease of 20.0±-17.3 mg/dl) randomly assigned to a diet-plus-exercise group, as compared to a control group (women had a decrease of 2.5±-16.6 mg/dl; men had a decrease of 4.6±-21.1 mg/dl).

5 **Stroke:** Physical activity exerts a positive effect in lessening the risk of stroke in men and women. Individuals who engage in moderate to high amounts of physical activity have a lower risk of stroke. Moderate to high levels of physical activity tend to lower blood pressure (if high); reduce body weight (if over fat); enhance vasodilatation of blood vessels (widening of the interior of blood vessels); improve glucose tolerance (how body breaks down

glucose); and promote cardiovascular health.

6 **Colon 11. Breast 12. Lung 13. Multiple Myeloma Cancers:** Moderate to vigorous physical activity has a greater protective effect than lower intensities of physical activity. Physically active men and women have a 30%-40% reduction in relative risk of colon cancer compared to their inactive counterparts. It seems that about 30-60 minutes of moderate to vigorous exercise per day is needed for this risk reduction, with higher levels of exercise showing even lower risk. In addition, physically active women have a 20%-40% reduction in relative risk of breast cancer compared to their inactive counterparts. Multiple myeloma cancer is more common in persons after the age of 50 and genetic damage occurs to plasma cells, transforming them into malignant or myeloma cells. Chronic fatigue is frequently reported and is a distressing side effect of multiple myeloma—as it is of many cancers. However, patients who walk 3-5 days per week for 15-30 minutes per session and do light resistance exercise (2-3 times per week) have demonstrated an increased overall quality of life.

7 **Osteoporosis:** It appears that resistance training and weight-bearing aerobic exercise may provide the needed stimulus for bone formation. Exercise programs to maintain and increase bone growth should be full-body in nature, including exercises such as squats and lunges, which direct the forces through the axial skeleton and allow for greater loads to be used. In addition, evidence does suggest that moderate weight-bearing activity, such as brisk walking done regularly, and on a long-term basis, is effective in averting age-related bone loss.

8 **Musculoskeletal Health and Sarcopenia:** Muscle mass, strength, power and endurance are essential contributing

factors for the improvement of musculoskeletal health and the enhancement of movement capabilities. Although these components of musculoskeletal health show substantial decreases with age, it has been suggested by research that this is due largely to a decrease in physical activity, and not solely to age.

Sarcopenia is the age-related loss of muscle mass and strength. Studies found that the rate of muscle loss with age is relatively consistent, approximately 1%-2% per year starting at age 50. For sarcopenia prevention, multi-joint exercises on machines are recommended, because these exercises require less skill and may allow the user to more easily control the exercise range of motion.

9 **Body Composition – Obesity :** The most favourable approach to weight loss is one that includes committed cardiovascular exercise, resistance training and caloric restriction within a sound behavioural-modification delivery program. Weight loss is achieved most effectively when cardiovascular exercise is increased up to 200-300 minutes of moderate-intensity activity accumulated over 5-7 days per week (which is equivalent to expending ≥ 2,000 kilocalories per week exercising). Resistance training and circuit training research has shown meaningful changes in body composition. One of the noteworthy benefits of resistance exercise, as it relates to body composition, is the positive impact of maintaining or increasing fat-free body mass while encouraging the loss of fat body weight in a progressive overload resistance training program.

10 **Arthritis:** Physicians commonly prescribe exercise as a treatment modality for arthritis. Consistent exercise improves aerobic capacity, muscle strength, joint mobility, functional ability and mood, without

apparent increases in joint symptoms or disease (Finckh, Iversen and Liang 2003). Exercise has been proposed to have a pain-relieving effect similar to that of a pharmacological treatment for somepeople. Designing the exercise for patients who have significant joint damage, especially in their weight-bearing joints, one has to keep it in mind that the high-impact exercise is contraindicated in many cases of arthritis and should be replaced with swimming, aquatic walking and biking, or other aquatic exercises which are much easier on the weight-bearing joints. Exercise programming for clients with arthritis should focus on gradually increasing cardiovascular conditioning, progressively overloading resistance exercise and steadily increasing flexibility and joint stability.

11 **Stress:** higher physical fitness is associated with lower levels of stress. It appears that the method of exercise that most benefits stress reduction is cardiovascular exercise. Research indicates that moderate-intensity aerobic exercise, performed 3 times a week (sessions lasting over 20 minutes) for up to 12 weeks, has the most influence on stress management.

12 **Mood State:** Some people said that they exercise because it makes them "feel good." Mood state is influenced by psychosocial, psycho-physiological, biochemical and environmental factors and it appears that cardiovascular and resistance exercise can positively affect various mood states, including tension, fatigue, anger and vigour. acute bouts of exercise may even improve a person's present mood state. It has been shown that a single bout of 25-60 minutes of aerobic exercise (at low, moderate or high intensities) increases positive mood feelings while decreasing a negative mood.

13 **Depression:** The antidepressant action is one of the most commonly accepted psychological benefits of exercise. Individuals with clinical depression tend to be less active than healthy ones. It also appears that both, acute exercise bouts and chronic exercise training programs have a positive effect on people with clinical depression.

Research does imply, though, that the greatest anti-depressive effects seem to occur after 17 weeks of exercise,although observable effects begin after 4 weeks. In addition, the effects of exercise on depression seem equal in both genders and are uninhibited by age or health status.

14 **Anxiety:** It appears that even short, 5 minute, bursts of cardiovascular exercise stimulate anti-anxiety effects. Research also indicates that individuals who train for periods of 10-15 weeks receive the greatest beneficial effects.

15 **Self-Esteem:** Exercise also has a positive influence on self-esteem. The effect appears to be more potent in those with lower self-esteem. Studies indicate that aerobic exercise may have a more pronounced effect than anaerobic exercise, but that may be because there is little research available on resistance training exercise and self-esteem. However, self - esteem is quite complex, and studies suggest that certain subcomponents, including perceived sport competence, physical condition, body image and strength, contribute to self-esteem. In relation to exercise, it is interesting to note that important factors influencing a person's self-esteem are perceptions of their body attractiveness and physical condition.

16 **The "Weekend Warrior":** They are the group which do physical activity once or twice in a week. "Weekend Warrior" exercisers who had no major risk factors (and

expended at least 1,000 kilocalories in this sporadic exercise pattern) had a lower risk of dying prematurely than their sedentary counterparts. However, individuals with one or more CHD risk factors may not benefit from this sporadic approach to physical activity, and should be encouraged to get their physical activity and exercise on most days, throughout the course of the week.

PRINCIPLES OF PHYSICAL FITNESS

Physical fitness falls into two separate categories - structured and unstructured. Structured means that you concentrate on a planned program of physical activity, usually to raise your fitness levels. Unstructured is a range of everyday activities that are done subconsciously and most of the time you are unaware that it is actually related to physical training. Doing things such as walking, climbing stairs, gardening, even standing up to change the channels on your T.V. you are effectively performing a squat and using the power of your legs to stand and sit.

Overload

In order to improve fitness whether it be cardiovascular or muscular the body needs to be stressed above what it normally encounters. This increase must be both systematic (to a planned program) and progressive to ensure performance gains without injuries. A majority of people when training tend to stay within their comfort zone. Therefore, the gains that they make are minimal.

In order for your body to progress to greater levels of fitness you must shock the system and place a higher demand on it more than it is normally used to. This can be done by increasing the intensity. For example, increasing the weight being lifted, the speed of which the exercise is being carried out, increasing your heart rate, the time spent on the exercise, increasing the distance and finally increasing the frequency at which you do it.

Recovery

Recovery is just as important as the hard work that you put into your training regime. There are several methods that may help enhance your recovery phase, these being massage, hydro-therapy, yoga, and reflexology all of which can help your body make the necessary repairs prior to moving onto the next training session. Just remember, no recovery, no improvement.

Progression

The principle of progression in exercise emphasises that a person should start slowly and increase exercise gradually. This will help avoid muscle soreness and minimise injuries. Progression in a training/fitness program should contain gradual increases in the number of repetitions, and the amount of time spent doing the exercise. The significance of progression is for exercise to be done gradually and to reduce the risk of overuse injuries, frustration and even burnout. When structuring an exercise program ensure the following acronym is used to ensure progression. F - Frequency, I - Intensity, T - Time, T - Type of exercise

Individuality

No two people are alike. Whether it be gender difference, race difference, or genetical difference when it comes to Physical Training we all have different requirements that need to be considered. Endomorphs (larger people) may not recover as quickly or have the same aerobic capacity as an Ectomorph (Thinner smaller build) and these individual differences need to be taken into account when evaluating a training program.

Specificity

Specificity is a principle in which specific kinds of exercise need to be used to develop specific parts of the body and specific elements of fitness. If you are an athlete and you play a sport then you will realise that you need to allocate training sessions to train for the specific sport that you play. For example it would be ineffective for a golf player to revolve his training around sprints when he could be using that valuable training time to concentrate on light resistance training, (weights) and technique training. Ensure your training sessions are of benefit to your particular sporting needs.

Variety

"Variety is the spice of life". Well, it also applies to fitness training. Some may say that this contradicts the fifth principle, specificity. However, it doesn't. By adding variety to your training regime you ensure that you don't plateau or stagnate due to a lack of interest. Even by changing running routes, venues where you train and a change in the exercise or activities that you perform on a regular basis will ensure that monotony doesn't set in.

In conclusion, these are only six of the basic principles of physical fitness, and many others can be found in other texts all of which will result in improving your fitness and lifestyle in general. It is not the mountain we must conquer, but ourselves.

WAIST HIP RATIO, LARGER HEART RATE, BMI AND TYPES AND PRINCIPLES OF EXERCISE(FIIT)

Waist to Hip Ratio: Two circumferences: waist and hip

Measures provide Cardio Vascular disease risk information

Men: 0.90 - 1.0+ = "high risk"

Women: 0.75 - 0.85+ = "high risk

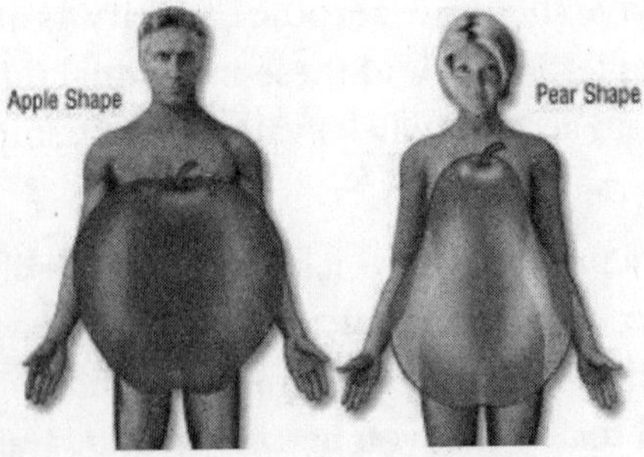

Abdominal body fat poses greater health risks than fat stored in other areas. Males who store more fat centrally have increased health risks associated with body fatness. Waist to Hip Ratio is an effective way to examine regional fat distribution

Waist-hip ratio or wast-to-hip ratio (WHR) is the ratio of the circumference of the waist to that of the hips. The waist-to-hip ratio is a quick, easy method to estimate body composition and describe body proportions. It is a common measure that reflects the degree of abdominal obesity a person exhibits.

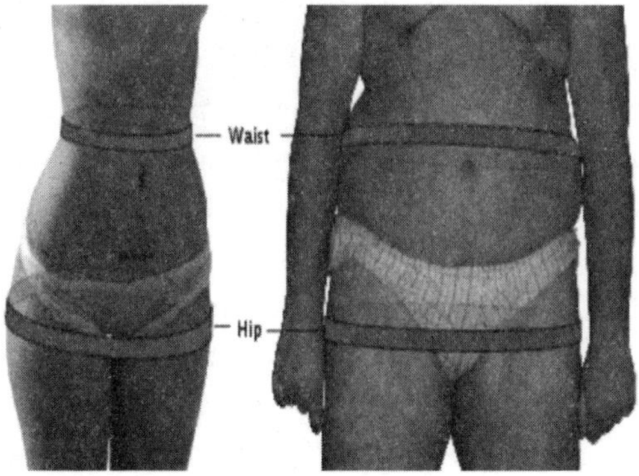

The waist circumference should be measured at the midpoint between the lower margin of the last palpable rib and the top of the iliac crest, using a stretch resistant tape that provides a constant 100% tension. Hip circumference should be measured around the widest portion of the buttocks, with the tape parallel to the floor.

The individual should stand with feet close together, arms at the side and body weight evenly distributed, and should wear little clothing. The subject should be relaxed, and the measurements should be taken at the end of a normal exhalation. Each measurement should be repeated twice;

if the measurements are within 1 cm of one another, the average should be calculated. If the difference between the two measurements exceeds 1 cm, the two measurements should be repeated.

Practically, however, the waist is more conveniently measured simply at the smallest circumference of the natural waist, usually just above the belly button, and the hip circumference may likewise be measured at its widest part of the buttocks or hip. Also, in case the waist is convex rather than concave, such as is the case in pregnancy and obesity, the waist may be measured at a horizontal level 1 inch above the navel. Some studies state that abdominal obesity is defined as a waist-hip ratio above 0.90 for males and above 0.85 for females, or a body mass index (BMI) above 30.0. Some findings show that women with waist-hip ratios of more than 0.8, and men with more than 1.0, are at increased health risk because of their fat distribution.

WHR has been found to be a more efficient predictor of mortality in older people than waist circumference or BMI. If obesity is redefined using WHR instead of BMI, the proportion of people categorized as at risk of heart attack, worldwide, increases threefold. The body fat percentage is considered to be an even more accurate measure of relative weight. Of these three measurements, only the waist-hip ratio takes account of the differences in body structure. Hence, it is possible for two women to have vastly different body mass indices but the same waist-hip ratio, or to have the same body mass index but vastly different waist-hip ratios.

WHR has been shown to be a better predictor of cardiovascular disease than waist circumference and body-mass index. However, other studies have found waist circumference, not WHR, to be a good indicator of cardiovascular risk factors, body fat distribution and hypertension in type 2 diabetes.

Fertility

A WHR of 0.7 for women and 0.9 for men has been shown to correlate strongly with general health and fertility. Women within the 0.7 range have optimal levels of estragon and are less susceptible to major diseases such as diabetes, cardiovascular disorders and ovarian cancers. Women with high WHR (0.80 or higher) have significantly lower pregnancy rates than women with lower WHRs (0.70-0.79), independent of their BMIs. Men with WHRs around 0.9, similarly, have been shown to be more healthy and fertile with less prostate cancer and testicular cancer.

Evidence suggests that WHR is an accurate somatic indicator of reproductive endocrinological status and long-term health risk. Among girls with identical body weights, those with lower WHRs show earlier pubertal endocrine activity.

These investigators report that a 0.1 unit increase in WHR decreases the probability of conception per cycle by 30% after adjustment for age, fatness, reasons for artificial insemination, cycle length and regularity, smoking, and parity.

Cognitive Ability

Some research studies found that a child's performance in cognitive tests were related to their mother's waist-hip ratio, a proxy for how much fat she stores on her hips. Children whose mothers had wide hips and a low waist-hip ratio scored highest, suggesting that foetuses benefit from hip fat, which contains a long chain polyunsaturated fatty acids, critical for the development of the foetus's brain. In addition, evidence suggests that children of low WHR teens were protected from the cognitive deficits often associated with teen birth.

Measure of attractiveness

The concept and significance of WHR as an indicator of attractiveness was first theorized by evolutionary psychologist Devendra Singh at the University of Texas at Austin in 1993.

Singh argued that the WHR was a more consistent oestrogen marker than the Bust-waist ratio (BWR) studied at King's College, London by Dr. Glenn Wilson in the 1970s.

Some researchers have found that the waist-hip ratio (WHR) is a significant measure of female attractiveness. Women with a 0.7 WHR are usually rated as more attractive by men from Indo-European cultures. Preferences may vary, according to some studies, ranging from 0.6 in China, South America, and some of Africa to 0.8 in Cameroon and among the Hazda tribe of Tanzania, with divergent preferences according the ethnicity of the observed being noted.

It appears that men are more influenced by female waist-size than hip-size: "Hip size indicates pelvic size and the amount of additional fat storage that can be used as a source of energy. Waist size conveys information such as current reproductive status or health status. In westernized societies with no risk of seasonal lack of food, the waist, conveying information about fecundity and health status, will be more important than hip size for assessing a female's attractiveness."

LARGER HEART RATE

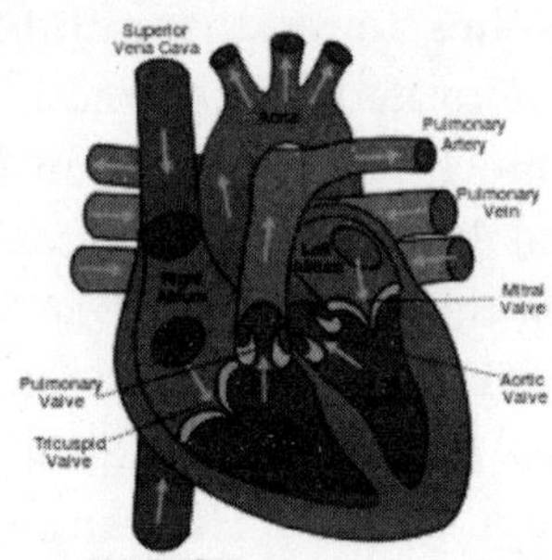

Athletic heart syndrome, (AHS) also known as athlete's heart, athletic bradycardia or exercise-induced cardiomegaly is a non-pathological condition commonly seen in sports medicine, in which the human heart is enlarged, and the resting heart rate is lower than normal. AHS is caused by significant amounts of aerobic exercise performed over a period of at least several months.

Athlete's heart is common in athletes who routinely exercise more than an hour a day, and occurs primarily in endurance athletes, though it can occasionally arise in heavy weight trainers. The condition is generally believed to be a benign one, but may sometimes be hard to distinguish from other serious medical conditions. For example, on the results of an electrocardiogram (EKG) the athletic heart syndrome may be mistakenly interpreted as evidence of serious heart disease.

Signs and symptoms - Athlete's heart most often does not have any physical symptoms, although an indicator would be a consistently low resting heart rate. Athletes with AHS often do not realize they have the condition unless they undergo specific medical tests. This is because athlete's heart is a normal, physiological adaptation of the body to the stresses of physical conditioning and aerobic exercise. People diagnosed with athlete's heart commonly display three signs that would usually indicate a heart condition if they were seen in a non-athlete: bradycardia, cardiomegaly, and cardiac hypertrophy. Bradycardia is a slower than normal heartbeat around 40-60 beats per minute. Cardiomegaly is the state of an enlarged heart. Cardiac hypertrophy is the thickening of the muscular wall of the heart, specifically the left ventricle, which pumps oxygenated blood to the aorta. In highly-trained athletes' bodies, more blood and oxygen are required by the peripheral tissues of the arms and legs. A larger heart results in higher cardiac output, as more blood is pumped out with each beat. The raised cardiac output allows the heart to beat more slowly (hence the bradycardia).

Another sign of the athlete's heart syndrome is an S3 gallop, which can be heard through a stethoscope. This sound can be heard as an irregularly shaped heart is filling with blood. The diastolic pressure creates a disordered flow of blood into the heart. However, if an S4 gallop is heard, the patient should be given immediate attention. An S4 gallop is a stronger and louder sound created by the heart if it is diseased in some way. It is typically a sign that there is a serious heart condition present in the athlete.

Cause: Athlete's heart is a result of dynamic physical activity such as aerobic training (more than 5 hours a week), rather than static training such as weight lifting. During intensive prolonged endurance or strength training, the body signals the heart to pump more blood through the body to counteract the oxygen deficit building in the skeletal muscles. Enlargement of the heart is a natural physical adaptation of the body to deal with the high pressures and large amounts of blood that can affect the heart during these periods. Over time, the body will increase both the chamber size of the left ventricle, and the muscle mass and wall thickness of the heart. Cardiac output, the amount of blood that leaves the heart in a given time period (i.e. litres per minute) is proportionate to both the chamber sizes of the heart and the rate at which the heart beats. With a larger left ventricle, the heart rate can decrease and still maintain a level of cardiac output necessary for the body. Therefore, it is very common for athletes with AHS to have lower resting heart rates than non-athletes.

The heart becomes enlarged, or hypertrophic, due to intense cardiovascular workouts, creating an increase in stroke volume, an enlarged left ventricle (and right ventricle), and a decrease in resting pulse along with irregular rhythms. The wall of the left ventricle increases in size by about 15-20% of its normal capacity. There is no decrease of the diastolic function of the left ventricle. The level of physical activity in a person determines what physiological changes the heart makes.

There are two types of exercise: Static (strength-training) and dynamic (endurance-training). Static exercise consists of weight lifting and is mostly anaerobic, meaning the body does not rely on oxygen for performance. It also moderately increases the heart rate and stroke volume (oxygen debt). Dynamic exercises are running, swimming, skiing, and cycling, which rely on oxygen from the body. This type of exercise also increases both heart rate and stroke volume of the heart. Both static and dynamic exercises involve the thickening of the left ventricular wall due to increased cardiac output, which leads to physiologic hypertrophy of the heart. It has been shown that once athletes stop training, the heart returns to its normal size. The following paragraph will give you an idea on how to find out Training Heart Rate(THR):

Maximum Heart rate - 220, if the age is 36 and resting pulse rate is 55

MHR - AGE - RESTING PULSE RATE = 220 - 36 - 55 = 129

70% of 129 = 129 x 70/100 = 90.3

90.3 + Resting Pulse Rate (55) = 145.3

85% of 129 = 129 x 85/100 = 109.65

109.65 + Resting Pulse Rate(55) = 164.65

Training Heart Rate = between 145.3 and 164.65

Diagnosis:

Athlete's heart is usually an incidental finding during a routine screening or during tests for other medical issues. An enlarged heart can be seen in echocardiography or sometimes on a chest X-ray. Similarities at presentation between athlete's heart and clinically relevant cardiac problems may prompt electrocardiography (ECG) and exercise cardiac stress tests.

It is important to distinguish between athlete's heart and hypertrophic cardiomyopathy, a serious cardiovascular disease characterized by thickening of the heart's walls, which produces a similar ECG pattern at rest. This genetic disorder is found in 1 out of 500 Americans and is a leading cause of sudden cardiac death in young athletes (although only about 8% of all cases of sudden death are actually exercise related)

10 Reasons Why a Large "Athlete's Heart" is Usually Not Dangerous

1 **Athlete's with large hearts tend to have an excellent heart function**

First, training that increases heart and coronary artery size generally improves the heart function or has no effect. Second, endurance athletes with large hearts tend to have as good or better heart and blood vessel functions compared to healthy non-athletes and other athletes. This is also true for football, handball, tennis, soccer, hockey, and basketball players. Athletes with enlarged hearts also tend to have better heart function during exercise, when the heart is under the most stress. This isn't surprising, but exercise tolerance is usually considered an excellent measure of heart function.

2 **Athlete's heart is not entirely permanent**

In many cases, athlete's heart reverses completely or considerably with de-training. Heart disease generally doesn't regress, at least not without surgery, drugs, or other treatments. Many of the changes in "athlete's heart" start to reverse themselves after just 8-12 weeks. Hearts of athletes even shrink during the rest season when they reduce their training levels. This would probably not happen if "athlete's heart" was a form of heart disease.

In highly trained athletes with more advanced "athlete's heart," however, the changes sometimes don't completely go away years after they stop training. They mostly regress, but not completely. This is especially true of endurance athletes, who usually have much larger hearts.

3 **Athlete's hearts are symmetrical and uniform**
In heart disease, certain patches of heart tissue often become disproportionately thicker or thinner. This is a sign the heart is being overwhelmed and may be failing. Certain chambers of athlete's hearts can become slightly larger than others. Runners often develop wider ventricles, and cyclists sometimes develop thicker heart walls, mainly due to differences in blood flow during these sports. Yet the thickness of the heart walls is still uniform and the other chambers are significantly larger in "athlete's heart".

4 **Athlete's hearts are wellvascularised**
Large athlete's hearts have greater blood vessel density than people with heart disease and healthy non-athletes. Athlete's hearts have increased vascularisation (more blood vessel density) compared to heart disease patients and sedentary people.
When athletes do have heart scarring, there is sometimes a decrease in perfusion — the ability to circulate blood through the heart. This kind of heart damage is rare for most athletes.

5 **Coronary arteries are generally larger in athletes**
People with heart disease also have enlarged coronary arteries. However, their arteries are disproportionately smaller compared to their hearts.

6 **Athlete's heart is not cumulative**
Athletes who keep training later in life have no significant further increase in heart size. The heart seems to increase in size to meet the demands of exercise, and no more.

7 **Athlete's with big hearts are usually asymptomatic**
Athletes with enlarged hearts rarely have obvious symptoms of heart disease, like chest pain, nausea, exercise intolerance, and trouble breathing. However, this doesn't

prove athlete's heart is not a sign of heart disease. Several studies have found that asymptomatic athletes can have extensive heart damage and atherosclerosis.

8 **Athlete's hearts usually have healthy mitochondria**

As the heart grows larger in heart failure, there is a decrease in mitochondrial density and function. In "athlete's heart," there is an increase in mitochondrial density and function of the heart and other muscles. This is one of the reasons moderate endurance training is used to help rehabilitate heart failure patients - it helps increase mitochondrial density and protect heart cells from dying.

9 **"Athlete's heart" is largely caused by different genes and signalling pathways than heart disease**

There are major differences in gene expression and molecular signalling between heart disease and "athlete's heart." In fact, many studies are looking at activating some of the same pathways that cause "athlete's heart" to prevent or treat heart disease.

10 **Elite athletes live a long time**

Elite athletes, of any kind, who often have enlarged hearts, tend to live longer than the average population. Interestingly, endurance athletes generally live the longest, despite usually having the largest hearts.

The studies that found elite athletes live longer didn't measure heart size, and it's possible that the athletes with the largest hearts were also the most likely to die. It is also possible that the reason these athletes lived longer was mainly due to other factors, but a recent review found that "lower cardiovascular disease mortality is likely the primary reason for their better survival rates.

BODY MASS INDEX

It is a method to find out a person`s obesity or fat accumulation.

Advantages of using BMI to classify obesity:

It is low-cost and easy to use for health professionals for assessing individuals.

It is commonly used to determine desirable body weights and allows people to compare their own weight status to that of the general population.

It correlates well with the amount of body fat as measured by more complex techniques.

It predicts dangers associated with obesity; as BMI increases the risk for diseases increases

It is a useful screening tool to use at the population level and, because it is universally accepted, BMI reference data is available for many different populations.

BODY COMPOSITION MUSCLE–BONE–FAT (EXAMPLE)

COMPOSITION	MEN-WT. 70 KG	HEIGHT 174 CM	WOMEN – WT 56 KG	HEIGHT 163 CM
TOTAL FAT	15%	10.5 KG	27%	15.12 KG
STORAGE FAT	12%	8.4 KG	16%	8.96 KG
ESSENTIAL FAT	3%	8.4 KG	12%	SEX SPECIFIC
MUSCLE	44.8%	31.3 KG	3.6%	2.02 KG
BONE	14.9%	10.4 KG	12%	6.7 KG
REMAINDER	25.3%	17.6 KG	25%	14 KG

Body Mass Index = Body Weight in Kg / Height in meters square. This formula will enable you to get the BMI and find out the obesity risk.

Normal : BMI 18 - 24.9

Overweight : 25 -29.9

Obese:> = 30

Class I : 30 - 34.9

Class II : 35 - 39.9

Class III:> = 40

You can Find the following fat percentage by using a simple method:

Present Fat

Fat mass

Lean Body Mass
Desirable Body Mass
Desirable Fat Loss 5%(example)
Body Mass Index(example for calculation)
Name = MR.X, Height = 170 cm, Weight = 66 KG, Skin fold Measurement of biceps = 10 mm and Sub scapular = 15MM so

find the following:

PRECENT FAT = BICEP FAT x .43 + SUBSCAPULAR FAT x .58 + 1.47 = .43 (it is a figure to add on) x 10 + .58(it is a figure to add on) x 15 + 1.47 = 14.47

FAT MASS = PRECENT FAT/100 x BODY WEIGHT = 14.47/100 x 66 kg = 9.55

LEAN BODY MASS(LBM) = BODY WEIGHT - FAT MASS = 66 - 9.55 = 56.45 kg

DESIRABLE BODY MASS(DBM) = LEAN BODY MASS / 1 -REDUCTION FAT = 56.45 / 1 - .05 = 56.45 / .95 = 59.42

BODY MASS INDEX = BODY WEIGHT(KG) / HEIGHT (MTR)2 = 66 KG / 1.70 MTR(2) = 22.83

BODY MASS INDEX (BMI) CHART

Weight in Kg and Height in Meter

	45kg	50kg	54kg	59kg	63kg	68kg	73kg	77kg	82kg	86kg	91kg	95kg	100kg	104kg	109kg	113kg
1.46M	22	25	26	29	31	34	36	38	40	43	45	47	49	52	54	56
1.47M	22	24	26	28	30	33	35	37	39	41	43	45	48	50	52	54
1.49M	21	23	25	27	29	31	34	36	38	40	42	44	46	48	50	52
1.50M	20	22	24	26	28	30	32	34	36	38	40	42	44	46	49	51
1.52M	20	22	23	25	27	29	31	33	35	37	39	41	43	45	47	49
1.55M	19	21	23	25	26	28	30	32	34	36	38	40	42	44	45	47
1.57M	18	20	22	24	26	27	29	31	33	35	37	38	40	42	44	46
1.60M	18	20	21	23	25	27	28	30	32	34	35	37	39	41	43	44
1.63M		19	21	22	24	26	28	29	31	33	34	36	38	40	41	43
1.65M		18	20	22	23	25	27	28	30	32	33	35	37	38	40	42
1.67M		18	19	21	23	24	26	27	29	31	32	34	36	37	39	40
1.70M			19	20	22	24	25	27	28	30	31	33	35	36	38	39
1.73M			18	20	21	23	24	26	27	29	30	32	34	35	37	38
1.75M			18	19	21	22	24	25	27	28	30	31	33	34	36	37
1.78M				19	20	22	23	24	26	27	29	30	32	33	35	36
1.80M				18	20	21	22	24	25	27	28	29	31	32	34	35
1.83M			16	18	19	20	22	23	24	26	27	28	30	31	33	34
1.85M			16		19	20	21	22	24	25	26	28	29	30	32	33

Healthy weight **Over weight** **Obese**

TYPES AND PRINCIPLES OF EXERCISE(FIIT)

Types of exercise

Physical exercises are generally grouped into three types, depending on the overall effect they have on the human body:

Flexibility exercises

such as stretching, improve the range of motion of muscles and joints.

Aerobic exercises: such as cycling, swimming, walking, skipping rope, rowing, running, hiking or playing tennis, focus on increasing cardiovascular endurance.

Anaerobic exercises: such as weight training, functional training, eccentric training or sprinting and high-intensity interval training, increase short-term muscle strength.

FITT principle of exercise

Frequency—How often (most/all days of week)

Intensity—How hard (55 - 90% of maximum heart rate)

Time—How long (duration Time: 30-80 minutes,

Gradually work up to this Start with brisk walking 10 min, 3-5 days/week

Work up to 60-80 min, most or all days/week)

Type—Mode of activity (aerobic, anaerobic, resistance etc.)

Overload can be achieved by increasing the resistance, increasing the intensity, increasing the number of sets, or increasing the number of repetitions.

Frequency:

As you might expect, this refers to how often you will exercise. After any form of exercise is performed your body completes a process of rebuilding and repairing. So, determining the frequency of exercise is important in order to find a balance that provides just enough stress for the body to adapt and also allows enough rest time for healing.

Intensity:

Defined as the amount of effort or work that must be invested in a specific exercise workout. This too requires a good balance to ensure that the intensity is hard enough to overload the body but not so difficult that it results in overtraining, injury or burnout.

Time:

Again, this is rather self-explanatory. Time is simply how long each individual session should last. This will vary based on the intensity and type.

Type: What type of exercise will you be doing? Will an exercise session be primarily cardiovascular, resistance training or a combination of both? And, what specific exercises will you perform.

Now you know the F.I.T.T. principle, planning a workout program and getting started should be a breeze. The F.I.T.T. guidelines for cardiovascular work and strength training are for cardiovascular benefits, they recommend exercising for a frequency of 3-5 times per week, at an intensity equal to 60-85 percent of your maximum heart rate for a time of 20-60 minutes. For strength training they recommend working out a minimum of two times per week at an intensity that is equal to 70-85 per cent of your one rep maximum (maximum weight you can use for one rep) for 8-10 reps and 1-3 sets. Planning a new fitness routine by breaking it into the four F.I.T.T. principle pieces allows you to quickly create a workout plan that will truly provide you with results.

For beginner exercisers choosing the Type of exercise may be the best place to start mapping out your routine. After all, if you have the perfect frequency, intensity and time, but hate the actual exercise then you'll never do it. So, start with something you like. This may be walking, biking, swimming or something else.

Next determine the Frequency. Consider how much time each week you truly will devote to this workout. Be realistic. There's no purpose in setting expectations so high that you likely will fail. Remember, the ACSM guidelines are 3-5 times per week, so a good start would be three days.

If you are very limited in your schedule then determining your Time would be the appropriate next step. Otherwise, choose your Intensity level, which will help determine how long your workout session should be. For example, a higher intensity will typically provide more benefit (such as burning more calories in a shorter amount of time). So, choosing to jog may require only 30 minutes of commitment versus walking which may require 45-60 minutes. Here's a quick example of both a cardiovascular and resistance workout program that utilizes the F.I.T.T. principle. Walk (Type) at 4 MPH (Intensity) for 45 minutes (Time) four times per week (Frequency). Perform exercises with dumbbells (Type) at 70% of your maximum 1 rep strength (Intensity) for 8-12 reps (Time) 3 times per week (Frequency).

Proverbs:

P stands for Progression. This simply means you start at a level you can handle and steadily progress from your baseline. R stands for Regularity. Exercise is recommended for most people at regular intervals of at least 3 times a week.

O stands for Overload. The effort must exceed the normal demands placed on the body. For example, if someone always takes the elevator, walking up stairs would exceed the normal demands the body is used to doing.

V stands for variety. Variety prevents boredom and challenges different aspects of the muscles.

R stands for Recovery. A recovery period allows the muscles to rest. You can alternate the type of exercises to allow for recovery. B is for Balance. An exercise program should not rely on one activity.

S is for Specificity. This just means to set a specific goal, with specific mini-goals intended to reach your target goal. For example, no one starts by running 5K. They begin with a goal to "walk one block," and increase the goal as each one is met.

STANDARD HEIGHT WEIGHT CHART FOR INDIAN MEN &WOMEN

Height in FEET AND METER	MEN – WEIGHT IN KGS	WOMEN – WEIGHT IN KGS
5`- 0" (1.523 Meter)	50.8 - 54.4	50.8 – 54.4
5`- 1" (1.548 Meter)	51.7 – 55.3	51.7 – 55.3
5`- 2" (1.574 Meter)	56.3 – 60.3	53.1 – 56.7
5`- 3" (1.599 Meter)	57.6 – 61.7	54.4 – 58.1
5`- 4" (1.624 Meter)	58.9 – 63.5	56.3 – 59.9
5`- 5" (1.650 Meter)	60.8 – 65.3	57.6 – 61.2
5`- 6" (1.675 Meter)	61.6 – 66.7	58.9 – 63.5
5`- 7" (1.700 Meter)	64.0 – 68.5	60.8 – 65.3
5`- 8" (1.726 Meter)	65.8 – 70.8	62.2 – 66.7
5`- 9" (1.751 Meter)	67.6 – 72.6	64.0 – 68.5
5`- 10" (1.777 Meter)	69.4 – 74.4	65.8 – 70.3
5`- 11" (1.802 Meter)	71.2 – 76.2	67.1 – 71.7
6`- 0" (1.827 Meter)	73.0 – 78.5	68.5 – 73.9
6`- 1" (1.853 Meter)	73.3 – 80.7	73.3 – 80.7
6`- 2" (1.878 Meter)	77.6 – 83.5	77.6 – 83.5
6`- 3" (1.904 Meter)	79.8 – 85.9	79.8 – 85.9

AVERAGE HEIGHT AND WEIGHT OF BOYS AT DIFFERENT AGE

AGE	WEIGHT IN KG	HEIGHT IN CM
Birth	3.3	50.5
3 Months	6.0	61.1
6 Months	7.8	67.8
9 Months	9.2	72.3
01 Year	10.2	76.1
02 Years	12.3	85.6
03 Years	14.6	94.9
04 Years	16.7	102.9
05 Years	18.7	109.9
06 Years	20.7	116.1
07 Years	22.9	121.7
08 Years	25.3	127.0
09 Years	28.1	132.2
10 Years	31.4	137.5
11 Years	32.2	140.0
12 Years	37.0	147.0
13 Years	40.9	153.0
14 Years	47.0	160.0
15 Years	52.6	166.0

AVERAGE HEIGHT AND WEIGHT OF GIRLS AT DIFFERENT AGE

AGE	WEIGHT IN KG	HEIGHT IN CM
Birth	3.2	49.9
3 Months	5.4	60.2
6 Months	7.2	66.6
9 Months	8.6	71.1
01 Year	9.5	75.0
02 Years	11.8	84.5
03 Years	14.1	93.9
04 Years	16.0	101.6
05 Years	17.7	108.4
06 Years	19.5	114.6
07 Years	21.8	120.6
08 Years	24.8	126.4
09 Years	28.5	132.2
10 Years	32.5	138.3
11 Years	33.7	142.0
12 Years	38.7	148.0
13 Years	44.0	150.0
14 Years	48.0	155.0
15 Years	51.5	161.0
16 Years	53.0	162.0
17 Years	54.0	163.0
18 Years	54.4	164.0

METHOD OF TRAINING - CONTINUES, INTERVAL, CIRCUIT, FARTLEK AND PLYOMETRIC

Continuous training is a type of physical training that involves activity without rest intervals It is divided into three parts (1) slow continuous running, (2) fast continuous training, (3) variable pace

(1) intensity will be low and heart beat 140-160/min. in slow continuous.
(2) intensity will be high and heart beat 160-180/min, duration will be 15-20minutes in fast continuous training.
(3) pulse rate 140-180/min and is a combination of both the running is at a variable pace.

This method of training improves aerobic fitness and is also a good way to burn body fat. The athlete runs, swims, cycles, rows for at least 30minutes.Overload is achieved by increasing the time, distance and speed.

Interval Training is a kind of training alternating between strenuous exercise and rest. The 'Rest' might mean milder exercise, e.g. 30m sprint 30m slow jogging. The 'Rest' periods give us time to recover. Interval training can be used to develop both aerobic and anaerobic fitness. Interval training is useful for swimming, rowing, running, cycling.

Circuit Training is made up 6 - 10 exercise stations at which a particular activity is performed. Circuit training develops the following qualities such as Cardio vascular fitness, muscular endurance, muscular strength and flexibility.

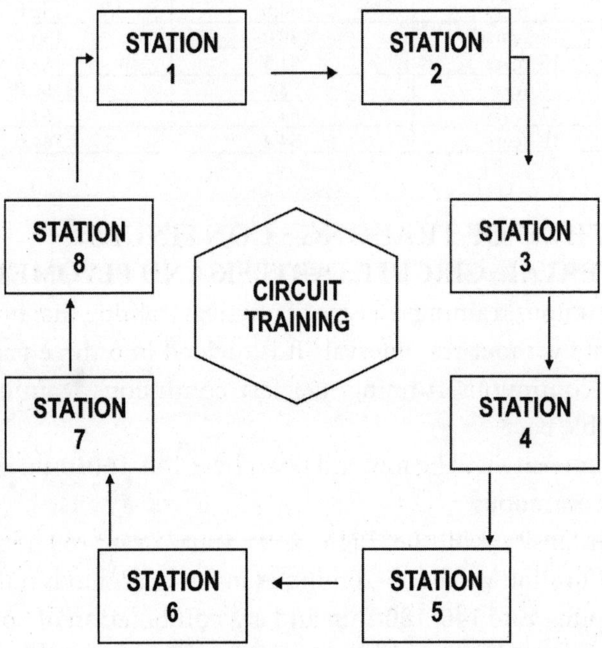

The word Fartlek is Swedish and means 'speed play' and this method of training involves many changes of speed, improves aerobic and anaerobic fitness. Fartlek training is very effective for games players, since games involve the ability to change pace. To overload increase the time or speed for each activity or choose more difficult ground. E.g. running uphill or on sand.

A typical Fartlek training:

Jog for warm up - 8 min

Sprint every other lamp post - 8 posts

Jog recovery - 5 mins

Sprint 10 paces - 10 reps

Recovery - 30 secs

¾ pace for ٣٠ sec - ٦ reps

Jog recovery - 1 min

Jog to finish - 10 mins

Plyometric

Speed and strength are integral components of fitness found in varying degrees in virtually all athletic movements. Simply put, the combination of speed and strength is power. For many years, coaches and athletes have sought to improve power in order to enhance performance.

Throughout the last century and no doubt long before, jumping, bounding and hopping exercises have been used in various ways to enhance athletic performance. In recent years, this distinct method of training for power or explosiveness has been termed plyometric. Whatever the origin of the word the term is used to describe the method of training that seeks to enhance the explosive reaction of the individual through powerful muscular contractions because of rapid eccentric contractions. When a concentric contraction occurs (muscle shortens) immediately following an eccentric contraction (muscle lengthens) then the force generated can be dramatically increased. If a muscle is stretched, much of the energy required to stretch it is lost as heat, but some of this energy can be stored by the elastic components of the muscle. This stored energy is available to the muscle only during a subsequent contraction. It is important to realise that this energy boost is lost if the eccentric contraction is not followed immediately by a concentric contraction.

To express this greater force the muscle must contract within the shortest time possible. This whole process is frequently called the stretch shortening cycle and is the underlying mechanism of plyometric training.

Type of Exercise	Examples	Intensity
Standing based jumps performed on the spot	Tuck Jumps Split Jumps Squat Jumps	Low
Forward jumps from standing	Bounds and hops over 10 to 20 meters	Low to Medium
Multiple double leg hops from standing	5 bounds 6 bunny hops Double footed jumps over hurdles Double footed jumps up steps	Medium
Multiple single leg jumps from standing start	Single leg hops up stadium steps	High
Drop jumps	2 x 6 jumps for height and distance	High
Speed bounds	4 x 20 meters	High
Multiple jumps with run up	3 x 2 hops and jump into sand pit with a 5 stride approach 2 x 10 bounds with a 5 stride approach	Very High

Upper Body

A variety of drills can be used to make the upper body more explosive:

Press ups and hand clap: Press-ups with a hand clap in between is a particularly vigorous way to condition the arms and chest. The pre-stretch takes place as the hands arrive back on the ground and the chest sinks, and this is followed quickly by the explosive upwards action.

Once again, to get the best training effect keep the time in contact with the ground to a minimum.

Medicine Ball: Another means of increasing upper body strength popular with throwers is to lie on the ground face up. A partner then drops a medicine ball down towards the chest of the athlete, who catches the ball (pre-stretch) and immediately throws it back. This is another high-intensity exercise and should only be used after some basic conditioning.

Planning a Plyometric Session

The choice of exercises within a session and their order should be planned. A session could:

- begin with exercises that are fast, explosive and designed for developing elastic strength (low hurdle jumps; low drop jumps)
- work through exercises that develop concentric strength (standing long jump; high hurdle jumps)

- finish with training for eccentric strength (higher drop jumps)

An alternative session could be:

- begin with low hurdle jumps
- progress to bounding and hopping, w continue with steps or box work
- finish with medicine ball work out for abdominals and the upper body

Warm up: A thorough warm up is essential prior to plyometric training. Attention should be given to jogging, stretching (dynamic), striding and general mobility especially about the joints involved in the planned plyometric session. A cool down should follow each session.

How many: It is wise not to perform too many repetitions in any one session and since it is a quality session, with the emphasis on speed rather than endurance, split the work into sets with ample recovery in between. An experienced athlete conducting lower body plyometrics may conduct up to 150-200 contacts in a session - athletes new to plyometric work should start with low to medium intensity exercises with around 40 contacts per session e.g. 2 sets of 6 bunny hops is 12 contacts. Similar approach should be taken with upper body plyometric. The focus must always be on quality and not quantity.

Recovery: Allow at least one minute of rest between each exercise repetition so as to allow the neuromuscular system to recover. Allow three days between plyometrics sessions when planning. Where to do it and what to wear: For bounding exercises use surfaces such as grass or resilient surfaces. Avoid cement floors because there is no cushioning. Choose well-cushioned shoes that are stable and can absorb some of the inevitable impact. All athletes should undergo general orthopaedic screening before engaging in plyometric training. Particular attention should be given to structural or postural problems that are likely to predispose the athlete to injury.

Conditioning for plyometric: Higher than normal forces are put on the musculoskeletal system during plyometric exercises so it is important for the athlete to have a good sound base of general strength and endurance. Most experts state that a thorough grounding in weight training is essential before you start plyometrics. It has been suggested that an athlete be able to squat twice their body weight before attempting depth jumps. However, less intensive plyometric exercises can be incorporated into general circuit and weight training during the early stages of training to progressively condition the athlete. Simple plyometric drills such as skipping, hopping and bounding should be introduced first. More demanding such as flying start single-leg hops and depth jumps should be limited to thoroughly conditioned athletes.

Summary: Plyometric type exercises have been used successfully by many athletes as a method of training to enhance power. In order to realise the potential benefits of plyometric training the stretch-shortening cycle (SSC) must be invoked. This requires careful attention to the technique used during the drill or exercise. The rate of stretch rather than the magnitude of stretch is of primary importance in plyometric training. In addition, the coupling time or ground contact time must be as short as possible. The challenge to you as coach or athlete is to select or create an exercise that is specific to the event and involves the correct muscular action. As long as you remember specificity and to ensure there is a pre-stretch first then the only limit is your imagination.

The following basic equipments are required to conduct a plyometric training program.

*Cones *Boxes *Hurdles or barriers *Stairs *Medicine

balls

There are six classifications to lower extremity plyometric exercises.

*Jump in place *Standing jumps *Multiple hops and jumps *Bounding *Box drill *Depth jumps

Effect of Training on VO2 MAX

VO2 MAX is the maximum amount of oxygen in millilitres, one can use in one minute per kilogram of body weight. For most of the sports including running events, VO2 Max is expressed as ml/kg/min-millilitres of O2 per minute per kilogram of body

weight. Cyclist and rowers tend to be measured strictly in term of litters of O2 per minute because body weight is less important in that sports. athletic performance is directly related to the efficiency of energy supplied to the muscles.

Energy system

(a) Aerobic Energy System

(b) Anaerobic Energy System

ATP (Adenosine Triphosphate): is a complex chemical compound formed with the energy released from food and stored in all cells, particularly muscles and only from the energy released by the breakdown of this compound can the cell perform work. Breakdown of ATP produces energy and ADP

Aerobic Energy System: ATP is manufactured from food mainly sugar and fat and this system produces ATP efficiently and is the prime energy source during endurance activities. Athletic performance is directly related to the amount of oxygen supplied to the muscles.

Anaerobic Energy System: PC(Phosphate-Creatine in muscle which when broken down aid in ATP formation

Anaerobic Glycol ysis: lactic acid system resulting from the incomplete breakdown of glucose/glycogen.

Factors Determining VO2 Max:

(A) Central-

(I) CVS

(ii) Respiratory System

(iii) Transports system(Blood Volume)

(B) Peripheral-

(i) Extent of capillarization

(ii) Mitochondrial No.

(iii) Enzymes

A (i) Cardio Vascular System(CVS):

Cardio output - Stroke Volume - Chamber size - Mil/min - Heart rate beat/min

A (ii)Respiratory system:

Lungs capacity(L/min) Diffusion capacity

Gas exchange surface area

A (iii)Transport system : Blood volume -5L - Haemoglobin(Hb%12-14gm%) - RBC 5.5million-PCV45%

Distribution system: Efficient nutrient,O2 delivery & waiste metabolite transfer & heat dissipation Extent of capillarization Reduceed distance of muscle fibre

Utilization system: Efficiency for extraction the oxygen(O2) by muscles No. of mitochondria Enzymes

Lactate Threshold

Lactic acid system is capable of releasing energy to re-synthesis ATP without the involvement of oxygen. Glycolysis (breakdown of carbohydrates)results in the formation of pyruvic acid &hydrogen ions(H+) and the build-up of H+ will make the muscle cells acidic and interfere with their operation. So carrier molecules called nicotinamide adenine dinucleotide (NAD+), remove the H+.

The NAD+ is reduced to NAD H which deposit the H+ at the electron transport gate (ETG) in the mitochondria to be combined with oxygen to form water (H2O). Insufficient oxygen then NAD H cannot release the H+ and they build up in the cell. To prevent the rise in acidity pyruvic acid accepts H+ and forming lactic acid which then dissociate into lactate and H+. Some of the lactate diffuses into the blood stream and takes some H+ with it as a way of reducing the H+ concentration in the muscle cell. The normal pH of muscle cell is 7.1, if the build-up of H+ continues and pH is

reduced to around 6.5, then muscle contraction may be impaired and the low pH will stimulate the free nerve endings in the muscle resulting in the perception of pain (burn). This point is often measured as the lactic threshold or anaerobic threshold or onset of blood lactate accumulation(OBLA). The normal amount of lactic acid circulating in the blood is about 1 to 2 milli moles/litter of blood. The onset of blood lactate accumulation (OBLA) occurs between 2 and 4 milli moles /litter of blood. The non- athletes the point is about 50% to 60% of VO2 Max and in trained athletes around 70% to 80% of VO2 Max.

Lactic Acid Friend or Foe

I t is responsible for burn in the leg muscles when exercising very fast and responsible for the soreness in the 48 hours following a session. A waste product to be re-synthesised by the liver (cori cycled) to form gloucose.

Improvement of Aerobic capacity

Enable the body to perform at a greater pace with a minimal amount of lactate, and more oxygen available to the working muscles and delay the onset of lactic acid at a given work intensity. Long and study runs, improve capillarization (formation of more blood vessels) and thus enhance the oxygen transport to the muscle. And also improve the efficiency in the heart and lungs.

Anaerobic Threshold

Lactic acid starts to accumulate in the muscles once you start operating above your anaerobic threshold. It is somewhere between 80% to 90% of maximum heart rate, in the trained athletes.

What you mean by low lactate threshold

It means not getting enough oxygen inside muscle cells. Inadequate concentration of enzymes.

Not having enough mitochondria in muscle cells.

Muscles, heart and other tissues are not very good at extracting lactate from the blood.

How to improve Lactate Threshold

Aim is to saturate the muscles in lactic acid which will educate the body`s buffering mechanism (alkaline) to deal with it more effectively.

Accumulation of lactate in working skeletal muscles is associated with fatigue of this system after 50 to 60 seconds of maximal effort.

Sessions should comprise of one to five repetitions (depends on the athletes ability) with near to full recovery.

Training continuously at about 85% to 90% of your maximum heart rate for 25 to 30 minutes will improve your LT. Once in a week and commence weeks before a major competition (buffering ability).

If lactate threshold is reached at low exercise intensity, it often means that the "oxidative energy system" in the muscles are not working very well.

Performing at a high level they would use oxygen to break lactate down to carbon dioxide and water thus preventing lactate from pouring in to the blood.

PHYSICAL FITNESS TEST BASED ON COMPONENTS

Event	Satisfactory	Good	Very Good	Excellent
MEN BELOW 30 YEARS				
2.5 Km Run	11.00 - 11.30 Min	-	10.29 - 10.00	9.59 and below
Push ups	21 - 30	31 - 40	41 - 45	46 and above
Sit ups	25 - 29	30 - 34	35 - 40	41 and above
300 meter run	55 - 59 sec	45 - 54 sec	44 - 47 sec	43 and below
30 - 40 YEARS				
Push ups	21 - 30	31 - 40	41 - 45	46 and above
2.5 Km Run	12.31 - 13.00 Min	12.00 - 12.30	11.30 - 11.59	11.29 and below
Push ups	16 - 24	25 - 31	30 - 35	36 and above
Sit ups	20 - 24	25 -30	31 -35	36 and above
300 meter	61 - 68sec	57 -60 sec	52 -56 sec	51 sec and below
MEN 40 - 45 YEARS				
2.5 Km Run	15.00 - 16.00 Min	13.00 - 14.59	12.31 - 12.59	Below 12.30
Push ups	10 - 17	25- 18	26 - 30	31 and above
Sit ups	15 - 19	20 -24	25 -32	33 and above
MEN 45 - 50 YEARS				
1.5 Km Run	12.00 - 12.59 Min	11.30 - 11.59	11.00 - 11.29	10.59 and below
Sit ups	15	16 - 20	21 - 25	26 and above
MEN 50 - 60 YEARS				
1.5 Km Run	15.00 - 14.01 Min	14.00 - 13.01	13.00 - 12.01	Below 12.00
WOMEN BELOW 30 YEARS				
1.6 Km Run	11.00 - 11.59 Min	09.00 - 10.59	07.00 - 08.59	Below 07.00 Min
Sit ups	13 - 17	18 - 22	23 -27	Above 27
60 meter Sprint	10.01 - 11 sec	09.01 - 10.00 sec	08.01 - 09.00 sec	Below 08.00 sec
WOMEN 30 -40 YEARS				
1.6 Km Run	11.30 - 12.30 Min	11.00 - 11.29	10.59 and below	

Sit ups	10 - 15	16 - 20	21 -24	
60 meter Sprint	12.01 - 13.00 sec	11.01 - 12.00 sec	11 and below	

EVALUATING STANDARD OF PHYSICAL DEVELOPMENT AND PHYSICAL FITNESS FOR INDIAN CHILDREN (BOYS)

Age	Grade	Height	Weight	30 Fly	Broad Jump	Balancing ability	6 x 10 shuttle run	800 M run	Vertical Jump	Ball throw
8Years	Satisfactory	127 - 133	24 - 28	5.3 - 4.8	164 - 183	15.8 - 14.7	10.5 - 11.5	212 - 210	25 - 29	372 - 442
	Good	134 - 139	29 - 32	4.7 - 4.5	184 - 193	14.6 - 13.6	17.4 - 16.5	209 - 187	30 - 34	443 - 513
	Excellent	>140	>33	<4.4	>194	<13.5	<16.4	<186	>35	>514
9 Years	Satisfactory	130 - 138	26 - 30	5.1 - 4.7	170 - 181	14.8 - 13.6	18.0 - 17.2	220 - 201	28 - 33	413 - 499
	Good	139 - 147	31 - 34	4.6 - 4.3	182 - 201	13.5 - 12.6	17.1 - 16.3	200 - 180	34 - 37	500 - 584
	Excellent	>148	>35	4.2 - 3.8	>20	<12.5	<16.2	<179	>38	>585
10 Years	Satisfactory	135 - 142	28 - 33	4.9 - 4.5	180 - 194	14.0 - 13.1	17.5 - 16.5	210 - 188	30 - 34	462 - 548
	Good	143 - 150	34 - 38	4.4 – 4.1	195 - 216	13.0 - 12.1	16.4 - 15.5	187 - 177	35 - 39	549 - 633
	Excellent	>151	>39	<4.0	>217	<12	<15.4	<176	>40	>634
11 Years	Satisfactory	140 - 149	31 - 36	4.8 - 4.4	189 - 204	13.5 - 12.6	17.1 - 16.2	204 - 185	35 - 39	502 - 596
	Good	150 - 157	37 - 41	4.3 – 3.9	205 - 225	12.5 - 11.6	16.1 - 15.4	184 - 166	40 - 44	597 - 691
	Excellent	>158	>42	<3.8	>226	<11.5	<15.3	<165	>45	>692
12 Years	Satisfactory	146 - 153	35 - 40	4.7 - 4.3	195 - 213	12.0 - 11.1	16.8 - 16.0	200 - 181	40 - 44	530 - 610
	Good	154 - 160	41 - 46	4.2 - 3.8	214 - 236	11.0 - 10.1	15.9 - 15.2	180 - 162	45 - 50	611 - 710
	Excellent	>161	>47	<3.7	>237	<10	<15.1	<161	>51	>711

EVALUATING STANDARD OF PHYSICAL DEVELOPMENT AND PHYSICAL FITNESS FOR INDIAN CHILDREN (GIRLS)

Age	Height	Height	Weight	30 Fly	Broad Jump	Balancing ability	6 x 10 shuttle run	800 M run	Vertical Jump	Ball throw
8Years	127 - 133	127 - 133		5.6 - 5.2	150 - 170	16.2 - 15.1	19.3 - 18.3	245 - 220	22 - 26	340 - 405
	134 - 141	134 - 141	27 - 30	5.1 - 4.7	171 - 180	15.0 - 14.1	18.2 - 17.2	219 - 200	27 - 33	406 - 470
	>142	>142	>31	<4.6	>181	<14	<17.1	<199	>34	>471
9 Years	129 - 136	129 - 136	25 - 30	5.4 - 4.9	164 - 180	15.5 - 14.1	19.0 - 18.0	235 - 210	26 - 30	358 - 444
	137 - 144	137 - 144	31 - 34	4.8 - 4.5	181 - 191	14.0 - 13.1	17.9 - 16.9	209 - 195	31 - 35	445 - 529
	>145	>145	>35	<4.4	>192	<13	<16.8	<194	>36	>530
10 Years	133 - 144	133 - 144	26.4 - 32.0	5.2 - 4.8	169 - 185	15.0 - 13.6	18.5 - 17.2	221 - 196	28 - 32	413 - 487
	145 - 156	145 - 156	33 - 38	4.7 - 4.3	186 - 200	13.5 - 12.6	17.1 - 16.2	195 - 182	33 - 37	488 - 563
	>157	>157	>39	<4.2	>201	<12.5	<16.1	<181	>38	>564
11 Years	144 - 153	144 - 153	33 - 39	4.9 - 4.6	180 - 195	14.5 - 13.1	18.0 - 17.0	218 - 190	32 - 36	472 - 551
	154 - 161	154 - 161	40 - 45	4.5 - 4.2	196 - 210	13.0 - 12.1	16.9 - 16.0	189 - 173	37 - 41	552 - 630
	>162	>162	>46	<4.1	>211	<12	<15.9	<172	>42	>631
12 Years	150 - 157	150 - 157	36 - 42	4.8 - 4.5	195 - 209	13.8 - 12.1	17.8 - 16.8	217 - 188	37 - 42	491 - 570
	158 - 163	158 - 163	43 - 48	4.4 - 4.0	210 - 224	12.0 - 11.1	16.7 - 15.8	187 - 169	43 - 47	571 - 650
	>164	>164	>49	<3.9	>225	<11	<15.7	<168	>46	>651

INDIAN MEN IDEAL HEIGHT - WEIGHT - AGE CHART (10% VARIATION ON EITHER SIDE OF AVERAGE ACCEPTABLE)

Ht. in CM	Age 15 -17	18 - 22	23 - 27	28 - 32	33 - 37	38 - 42	43 - 47	48 & above
152	Kg 46.0	47.0	49.0	50.0	51.0	52.0	52.5	53.0
154	Kg 47.0	48.0	50.0	51.5	52.5	53.0	53.5	54.0
156	Kg 48.0	49.0	51.0	52.5	53.5	54.0	54.5	56.0
158	Kg 49.0	50.0	52.0	54.0	55.0	55.5	56.0	56.5
160	Kg 50.0	51.0	53.0	55.0	56.0	56.5	57.0	57.5
162	Kg 51.0	52.5	54.5	56.0	57.5	58.0	58.5	59.0
164	Kg 52.0	53.5	55.5	57.5	59.0	59.5	60.0	60.5
166	Kg 53.5	55.0	57.0	59.0	60.5	61.5	61.5	62.0
168	Kg 55.5	56.5	58.5	60.5	62.0	63.0	63.5	64.0
170	Kg 56.5	58.0	60.0	62.0	64.0	64.5	65.0	65.5
172	Kg 58.0	60.0	61.5	63.5	65.0	66.0	66.5	67.5
174	Kg 59.5	61.0	63.5	65.5	67.5	68.0	68.5	69.0
176	Kg 61.0	62.5	65.0	67.0	69.0	69.5	70.0	71.0
178	Kg 62.5	64.0	66.5	68.5	70.5	71.5	72.0	72.5
180	Kg 64.0	65.5	68.0	70.5	72.5	73.0	74.0	74.5
182	Kg 66.0	67.5	69.5	72.0		75.0	75.5	76.5
184	Kg 67.0	70.0	71.5	74.0	76.0	76.5	77.5	78.0
186	Kg 69.0	70.5	73.0	75.5	78.0	78.5	79.0	80.0
188	Kg 70.5	72.0	75.0	77.5	79.5	80.0	81.0	82.0
190	Kg 72.0	73.5	76.0	78.5	80.5	81.0	82.0	83.0

Chapter IV
YOGA EDUCATION

MEANING AND HISTORY OF YOGA

The meaning of 'yoga' is so expansive and fluid that it can simultaneously connect the beliefs of many and mean something subtly different to every practitioner. It may mean holding a position or remaining in union with God. In either case, yoga is both the means and the end.

Yoga is more than mastering postures and increasing your flexibility and strength.

"The traditional purpose of Yoga, however, has always been to bring about a profound transformation in the person through the transcendence of the ego. "In Hinduism, Buddhism and Jainism the word yoga means "spiritual discipline". People often associate yoga with the postures and stances that make up the physical activity of the exercise, but after closer inspection it becomes clear that there are many more aspects of yoga. It is an activity that has been practiced for thousands of years, and it is something that has evolved and changed overtime. Different factions of yoga have developed since its conception.

The exact history and origins of yoga are uncertain. However, there are pieces that have been connected and allow us to make some conclusions. It is known that yoga originated in the East. The earliest signs of yoga appear in ancient Shamanism. Evidence of yoga postures were found on artefacts that date back to 3000 B.C. Evidence of yoga is found in the oldest-existing text, Rig-Veda. Rig-Veda is a composition of hymns. Topics of the Rig-Veda include prayer, divine harmony, and greater being. "The primary goal of shamanism was to heal members of the community and act as religious mediators". Yoga originally focused on applying and understanding the world. Its focus later changed to the self. Self-enlightenment became the ultimate goal.

Modern Yoga

Modern yoga is based on five basic principles that were created by Swami Sivananda.

- Proper relaxation
- Proper exercise
- Proper breathing
- Proper diet
- Positive thinking and meditation

Astanga Yoga and types of yoga: Though there are multiple origins attributed to Ashtanga yoga in general, this important form of yoga consists of some specific ideas related to the body poses that are used. Ashtanga yoga includes an "eight limbed" system, where a collection of eight separate and unique concepts provides an overall discipline for this type of yoga. Ashtanga Vinyasa Yoga, also known as Ashtanga Yoga, is a style of yoga founded and popularized by K. Pattabhi Jois, and which is often promoted as a modern-day form of classical Indian yoga. Pattabhi Jois began his yoga studies in 1927 at the age of 12, and by 1948 had established an institute for teaching the specific yoga practice known as Ashtanga "eight-limbed")

Vinyasa Yoga. Ashtanga Vinyasa Yoga is named after the eight limbs of yoga mentioned in the Yoga Sutras of Patanjali. Power Yoga and Vinyasa Yoga are generic terms that may refer to any type of vigorous yoga exercise derived from Ashtanga Vinyasa Yoga. The sage Patanjali outlined eight aspects or "limbs" of spiritual yogic practice in his Yoga Sutras:

Sanskrit	English
Yama	moral codes
Niyama	self-purification and study
Asana	posture
Pranayama	breath control
Pratyahara	withdrawing of the mind from the senses
Dharana	concentration
Dhyana	deep meditation
Samadhi	union with the object of meditation

The first four limbs—yama, niyama, asana and pranayama—are considered external cleansing practices. According to Pattabhi Jois, defects in these external practices are correctable while defects in the internal cleansing practices—pratyahara, dharana, dhyana and samadhi—are not. Pattabhi Jois thought these internal defects to be potentially dangerous to the mind unless the correct Ashtanga Vinyasa Yoga method was followed.

Higher level practices within Ashtanga

Bandhas: There are three bandhas which are considered our internal body locks, prescribed in the different asanas. The bandha is a sustained contraction of a group of muscles that assists the practitioner not only in retaining an asana but also in moving in and out of it.

(a) The Mūla Bandha, or root lock, is performed by tightening the muscles around the pelvic and perineum area.

(b) The U īyāna Bandha, often described as bringing the navel to the base of the spine, is a contraction of the muscles of the lower abdominal area - this bandha is considered the most important bandha as it supports our breathing and encourages the development of strong core muscles.

(c) Jālandhara Bandha, throat lock, is achieved by lowering the chin slightly while raising the sternum and the palate bringing the gaze to the tip of the nose.

Drishtis

Drishti (drsti), or focused gaze, is a means for developing concentrated intention. The most common is Ūrdhva, or upward gazing, where the eyes are lifted, with the spine aligned from crown to tailbone. This technique is employed in a variety of asanas. There are, in total, nine drishtis that instruct the yoga student in directing his or her gaze. Each asana is associated with a particular drishti. They include:

- **A gu ha madhyai:** to the thumb
- **Bhrūmadhya:** to the third eye, or between the eyebrows
- **Nāsāgrai:** at the tip of the nose (or a point six inches from the tip)
- **Hastagrai:** to the palm, usually the extended hand
- **Pārśva:** to the left/right side
- **Ūrdhva:** to the sky, or upwards l Nābhicakra: to the navel
- **Pādayoragrai:** to the toes

Mantras: The Ashtanga practice is traditionally started with the following Sanskrit mantra:

vande gurū ā cara āravinde sa darśitasvātmasukhāvabodhe ni śreyase jā galikāyamāne sa sāra hālāhala mohaśāntyai ābāhu puru ākāra śa khacakrāsi dhāri am sahasra śirasa śvetam pra amāmi patañjalim

which is roughly translated into English as:

I bow to the lotus feet of the gurus, The awakening happiness of one's own self revealed, Beyond better, acting like the jungle physician, Pacifying delusion, the poison of samsara. Taking the form of a man to the shoulders, Holding a conch, a discus, and a sword, One thousand heads white, To Patanjali, I salute. and closes with the **mangala mantra:**

ssvasti prajābhya paripālayantā nyāyena mārge a mahī mahīśā

gobrāhma ebhya śubhamastu nitya lokā samastā sukhino bhavantu

which is roughly translated into English as:

May prosperity be glorified, may rulers (administrators) rule the world with law and justice, may divinity and erudition be protected. May all beings be happy and prosperous. A more **literal translation:** May it be well with the people. Let Earth's rulers protect the Earth with the path of law and justice. May good fortune always befall cows and Brahmins. May all the worlds be happy and comfortable?

TYPES OF SURYA NAMASKAR AND THE TECHNIQUE OF PRANAYAMA

Step 1 Surya Namaskar Type A, Version 1 is Pranamasana -Prayer Pose

1 Stand upright at the top of your mat with your feet together, big toes touching, and close your eyes.
2 Bend your elbows, relax them by your sides and place the palms of your hands together in Pranamasansa - prayer pose, also known as the yoga hand position Namaskara Mudra.
3 Relax your shoulders. Stand with proper posture so the crown of your head radiates to the sky.
4 Breathe normally.

Step 2 Surya Namaskar Type A, Version 1 is Hasta Utthanasana - Raised Arms Pose

1 Open your eyes.
2 Separate the palms of your hands and INHALE as you straighten your elbows as you reach towards the sky.
3 Keep your arms shoulder-width apart and gently flex your wrists so you fingers are pointing behind you.
4 Relax your head back to look at your thumbs, which brings you into a slight back bend. Relax your shoulders away from your ears.

Step 3 Surya Namaskar Type A, Version 1 is **Padahastasana -Hand to Foot Pose**

1 EXHALE and forcibly contract your abdominal muscles as you hinge at your hips to bend forward and bring your nose as close to your knees, or shins, as possible. Keep your arms by your ears.
2 Touch your fingertips, or palms of your hands to the floor. Place the tips of your fingers in line with the tips of your toes.
3 As your bending over, keep a flat back until your upper body is parallel with the floor. Then, round your back as necessary to get into the proper position. Knees are straight, quadriceps are contracted.

Step 4 Surya Namaskar Type A, Version 1 is Ashwa Sanchalasana - Equestrian Pose

1 Place your all your fingertips on the floor, keeping them in line with the tips of your toes - bending your knees to do this if you have to. Fingers together and pointing forward, arms straight.
2 INHALE as you take a big step back with your right foot so your right leg is fully extended behind you, while at the same time bending your left knee. Do not bend your knee past the tips of your left toes.
3 Bend your right knee to rest your right shin on the floor

and extend your ankle to rest the top of your foot on the floor. You can keep your foot flexed and toes on the floor if you like.

4 Tilt your head back by looking up and relax your shoulders.

Ashwa Sanchalasana, Equestrian Pose

Step 5 Surya Namaskar Type A, Version 1 is Adho Mukha Svanasana - Downward Dog

Downward Dog may look simple, but it's a complex yoga pose. I provide an additional link at the bottom of the page so you can

read another, more detailed, description from the Yoga Journal.

1 Flex your right ankle to come up onto the tips of your right toes and straighten your right knee so your shin comes off the mat.

2 Place your palms flat on the floor with your fingers spread apart, EXHALE and extend your left foot back to meet your right foot.

3 Lift your hips into the air so you make a triangle with the floor.

4 Straighten your arms. Reach your heels towards the floor.

5. Look at your navel and relax your neck.

Downward Dog

Step 6 Surya Namaskar Type A, Version 1 is Ashtanga Namaskara - Salute with 8 Points

1 Hold your breath as you lower your knees, chin and chest to touch the floor in that order.
2 Keep your hands and feet in the same position and bend your elbows.
3 Look forward.
4 The eight points are your chin, chest, 2 hands, 2 knees and 2 feet.

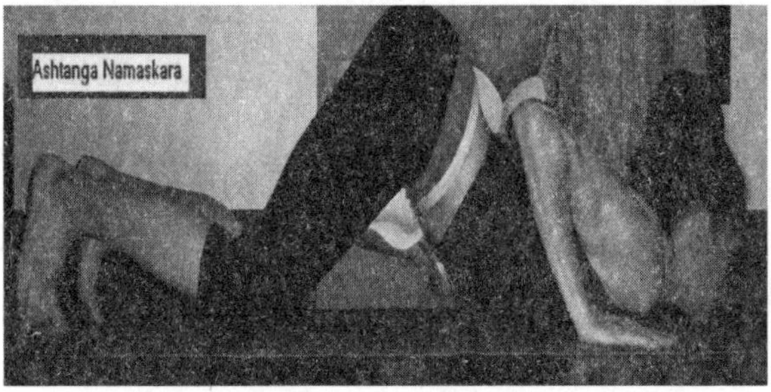

8-Points Pose, Ashtanga Namaskara

Step 7 Surya Namaskar Type A, Version 1 is Bhujangasana -Cobra Pose

1 Keep your hands and feet in the same place.
2 INHALE and point your toes to place the tops of your feet on the floor and push your body forward so your knees

are almost straight and your hips rest on the floor.

3 Look up and bend your head back as you use your hands to lift your shoulders, and possibly your rib cage, off the floor with a slight back bend.

4 Hug your elbows close to your ribcage and relax your leg muscles.

Cobra Pose 75

Step 8 Surya Namaskar Type A, Version 1 is Adho Mukha Svanasana - Downward Dog

1. EXHALE, straighten your arms flex your feet and lift your hips into the air so you make a triangle with the floor.

2.Reach your heels towards the floor.

3. Look at your navel and relax your neck.

Step 9 Surya Namaskar Type A, Version 1 is Ashwa Sanchalasana

1 INHALE as you step your right foot forward so your fingertips are even with the tips of your toes.

2 Your left leg is fully extended behind you. Do not bend your right knee past the tips of your left toes.

3 Bend your left knee to rest your left shin on the floor and extend your ankle to rest the top of your foot on the floor. You can keep your foot flexed and toes on the floor if you like.

4 Tilt your head back by looking up and relax your shoulders.

Step 10 Surya Namaskar Type A, Version 1 is Pasahastasana — Hand to Foot Pose

1 EXHALE and forcibly contract your abdominal muscles as you step your left foot forward together with your right foot into a forward bend. Bring your nose as close to your knees, or shins, as possible.

2 Place the tips of your toes in line with the tips of your fingers.

Step 11 Surya Namaskar Type A, Version 1 is Hasta Utthanasana - Raised Arms Pose

1 INHALE as you come back to a standing position with a flat back and reach towards the sky.

2 Keep your arms shoulder-width apart and gently flex your wrists so you fingers are pointing behind you.

3 Relax your head back to look at your thumbs, which brings you into a slight back bend. Relax your shoulders away from your ears.

Step 12 Surya Namaskar Type A, Version 1 is Pranamasana -Prayer Pose

1 Bend your elbows, relax them by your sides and place the palms of your hands together in pranamasansa - prayer pose, also known as the yoga hand position namaskara mudra. Close your eyes.

2 Stand upright at the top of your mat with your feet together, big toes touching.

3 Relax your shoulders. Stand with proper posture so the crown of your head radiates to the sky.

4 Breathe normally.

How to do Pranayam

- **Bhastrika Pranayam:** Bellows Breath
- **Kapalbhati Pranayam:** Shining Forehead
- **Breath Anulom Vilom Pranayam:** Alternate Nostril
- **Breath Bahya Pranayam:** External Breath

- **Bhramari Pranayam:** Bee Breath
- **Udgeeth Pranayam:** Chanting Breath

Pranayam (also spelled Pranayama) is an ancient practice concerned with breath control. Research has shown that practicing Pranayama can relieve symptoms of asthma. It is also beneficial in treating stress related disorders, such as anxiety and depression. There are a total of six types of Pranayam practice, all of which are detailed here.

1 of 6: Bhastrika Pranayam: Bellows Breath

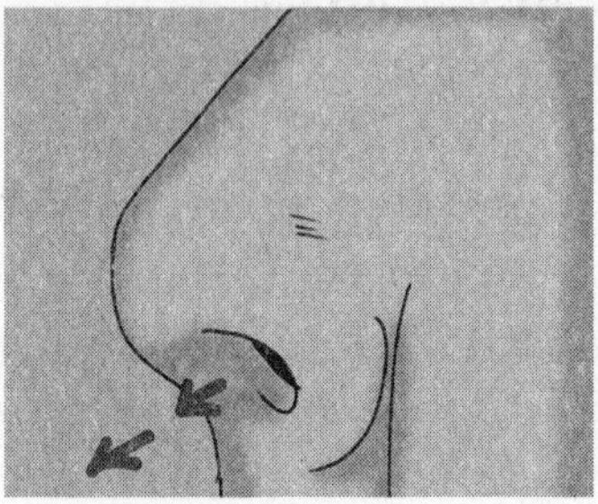

1. Breath-in deeply through your nostrils. First, feel the diaphragm move down, allowing the lungs to expand and forcing the abdomen out; then feel your chest expand with your collar bones rising last.

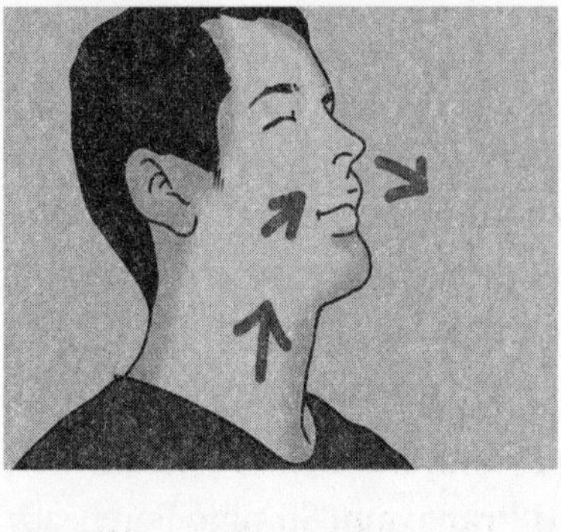

2. Breath out quickly through your nostrils. Feel the collar bones dropping, chest deflating, and abdomen shrinking as the lungs collapse. This process of exhaling should be much faster than the process of inhaling - almost like a rapid deflation.

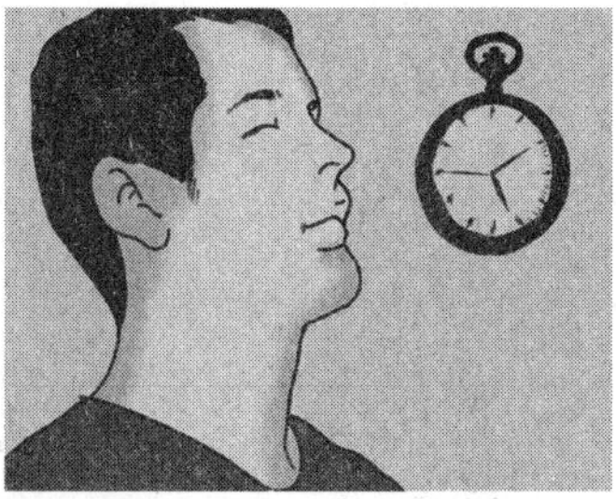

3. Repeat the process. When correctly done, your chest will expand when you breathe in and deflate when you breathe out. Continue doing this for 5 minutes.

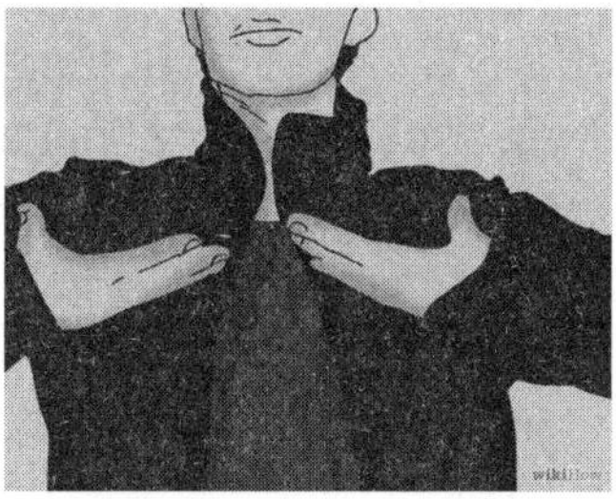

4. with practice, speed up your breathing. Beginners should always start slowly to avoid hyperventilating, but over time, it will be possible to turn this into a rapid breathing technique

2of 6: Kapalbhati Pranayam: Shining Forehead Breath

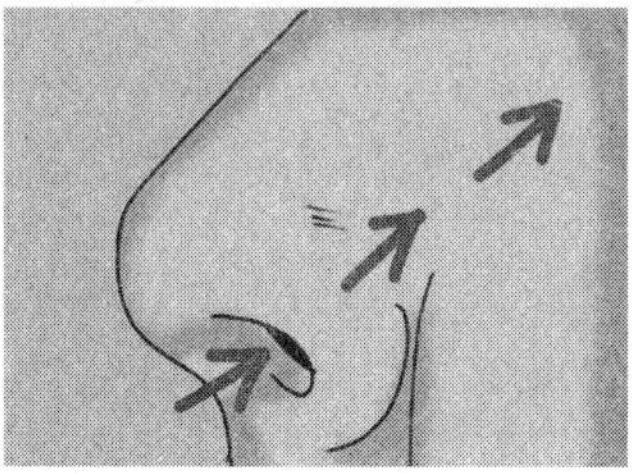

1. Inhale through your nostrils normally until your lungs are full. Keep your inhalation slow but unforced. First, feel the diaphragm move down, allowing the lungs to expand and forcing the abdomen out; then feel your chest expand with your collar bones rising last.

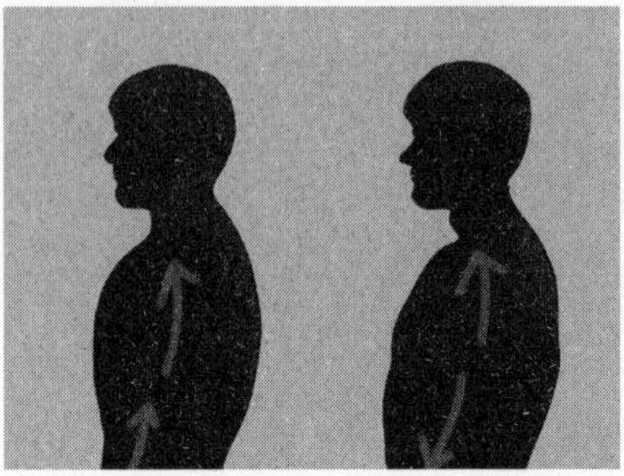

2. Exhale through both nostrils forcefully. This places the emphasis of the breath on the exhale rather than the (natural) inhale. Assist your exhalation by pulling in your stomach muscles to expel air. Exhaling should take much less time than it took to inhale. "Forced" exhalation means that the contraction of your stomach muscles helps push the air out of your body. It does not mean that the exhalation should be uncomfortable for you in any way.

3.Repeat breaths for 15 minutes. You may take a minute's rest after every five minutes.

3 of 6: Anulom Vilom Pranayam: Alternate Nostril

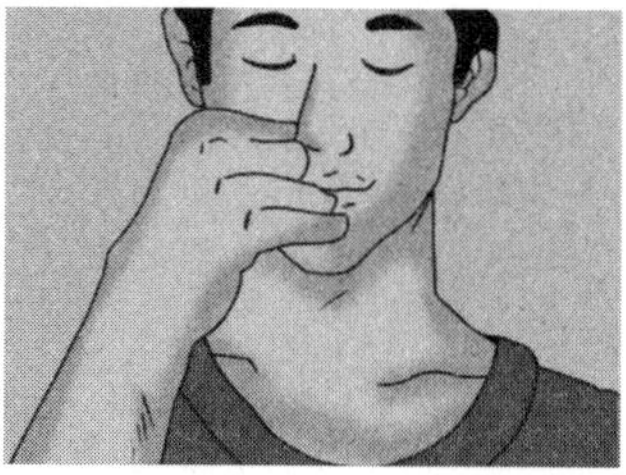

1 Close your eyes. Focus your attention on your breathing.
2 Close the right nostril with the right thumb. Simply press the thumb against your nostril to block it.
3 Inhale slowly through the left nostril. Fill your lungs with air. First, feel the diaphragm move down, allowing the lungs to expand and forcing the abdomen out; then feel your chest expand with your collar bones rising last.
4 Remove your thumb from your right nostril. Keep your right hand by your nose and your lungs full of air.

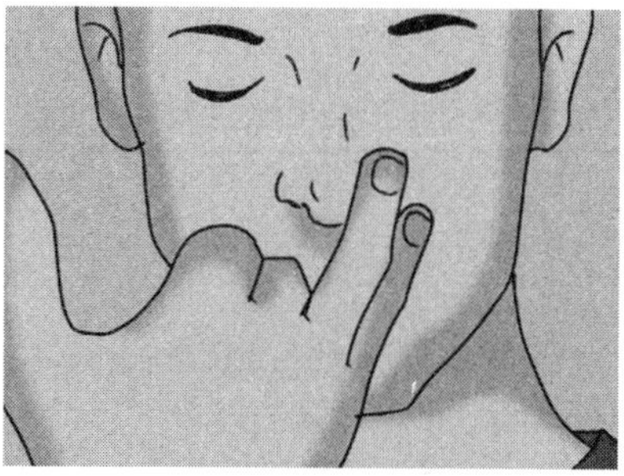

5 Use your ring and middle finger to close your left nostril. Most people find it easier to continue using the same hand to block either nostril, but you're welcome to switch hands depending on which nostril you're blocking. You can also switch if your arm gets tired.
6 Exhale slowly and completely with the right nostril. Feel the collar bones dropping, chest deflating, and abdomen shrinking

as the lungs collapse. When you've finished exhaling, keep your left nostril closed.

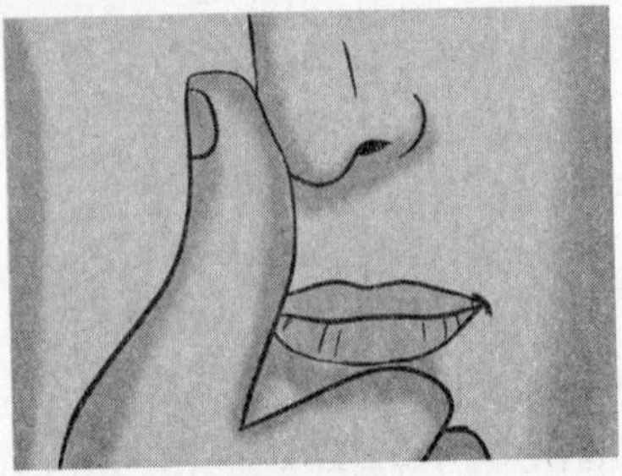

7. **Inhale** through the right nostril. Fill your lungs.

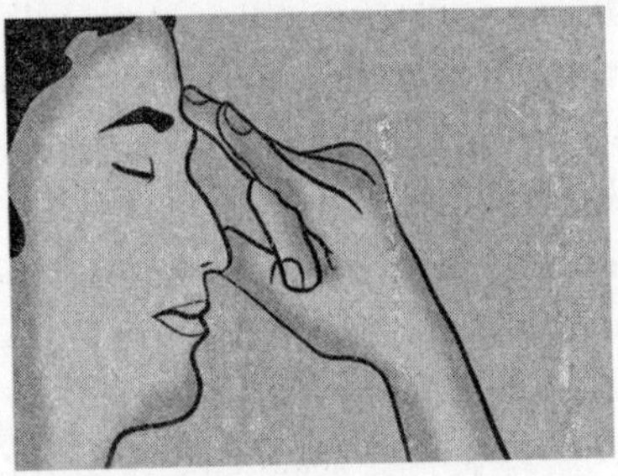

8. **Breath out** slowly through the left nostril. This process is one round of Anulom Vilom Pranayam.

9.**Continue for** 15 minutes. You may take a minute's rest after ev ery five minutes of exercise.

4 of 6: Bahya Pranayam: External Breath

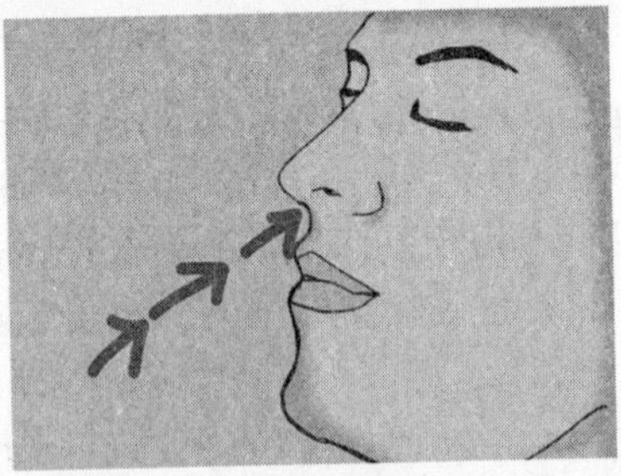

1. Inhale deeply through your nose. First, feel the diaphragm move down, allowing the lungs to expand and forcing the abdomen out; then feel your chest expand with your collar bones rising last.
2. Exhale forcefully. Use your stomach and diaphragm to push the air from your body. "Forced" exhalation means that the contraction of your stomach muscles helps push the air out of your body. It does not mean that the exhalation should be uncomfortable for you in any way.
3. Touch your chin to your chest and suck in your stomach completely. The goal is to leave a hollow below your ribcage, making it look like the front muscle wall of your abdomen is pressed against the back. Hold this position - and your breath - for as long as is comfortable.
4. Lift your chin and breathe in slowly. Allow your lungs to completely fill with air.
5. Repeat 3 to 5 times.

5 of 6: Bhramari Pranayam: Bee Breath

1.Close your eyes. Focus on your breathing.

2. Place your thumbs in your ears, your index fingers above your eyebrows, and your remaining along the sides of your nose. Keep each pinky finger near a nostril.

3. Breath in deeply through the nose. First, feel the diaphragm move down, allowing the lungs to expand and forcing the abdomen out; then feel your chest expand with your collar bones rising last.

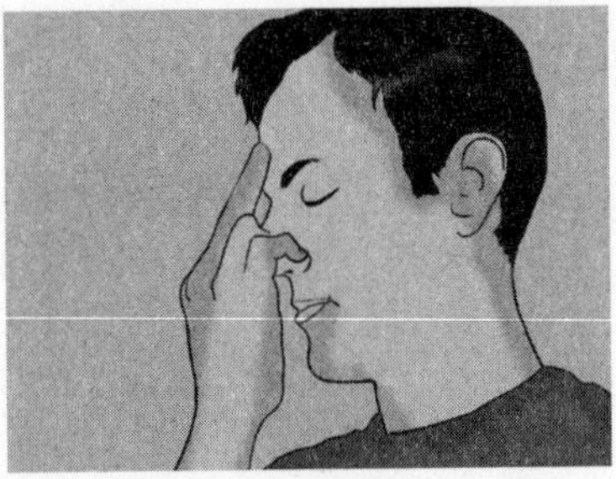

4. Use your pinkies to partially close each nostril. Keep your lungs filled

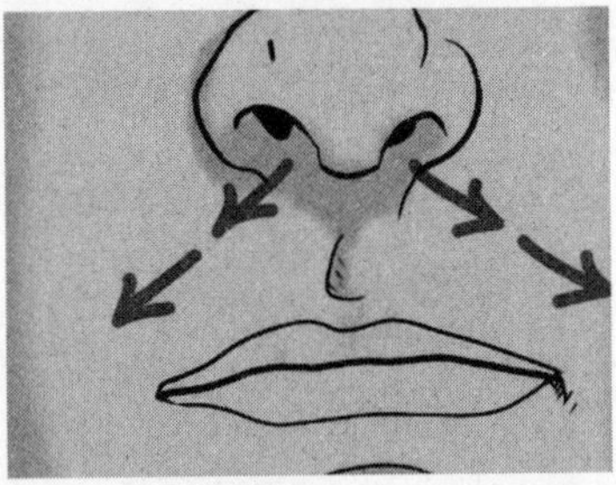

5. Breath out through the nose while humming. Note that

the humming sound should originate in your throat, not as a result of your partially-blocked nostrils.

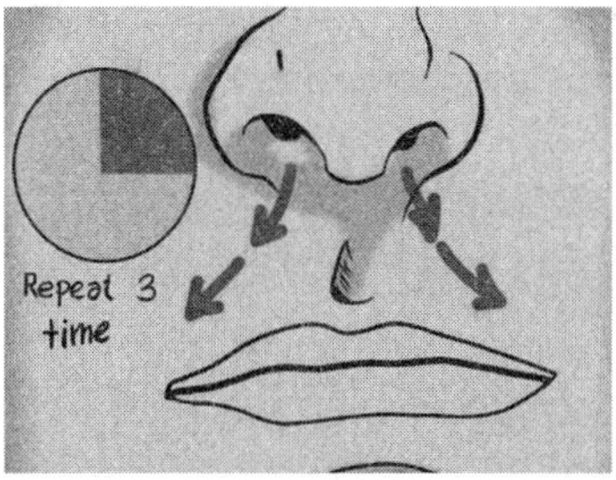

6. Repeat three times.

6 of 6: Udgeeth Pranayam: Chanting Breath

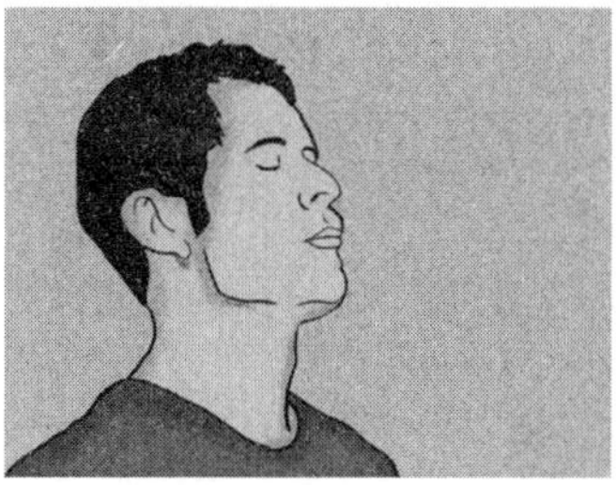

1. Breath in deeply through the nose. First, feel the diaphragm move down, allowing the lungs to expand and forcing the abdomen out; then feel your chest expand with your collar bones rising last.

2. Exhale very slowly while saying Om. Allow the syllable to draw out as slowly as you can. Make sure to keep the O long and the M short. ("OOOOOOm.")

3. Repeat 3 times.

BENEFIT OF YOGA

Weight loss, a strong and flexible body, glowing beautiful skin, peaceful mind, good health - whatever you may be looking for, yoga has it on offer. However, very often, yoga is only partially understood as being limited to asanas (yoga poses). As such, its benefits are only perceived to be at the body level and we fail to realize the immense benefits yoga offers in uniting the body, mind and breath. When you are in harmony, the journey through life is calmer, happier and more fulfilling.

With all this and much more to offer, the benefits of yoga are felt in a profound yet subtle manner. Here, we look at the top 10 benefits of regular yoga practice.

1 All-round fitness. You are truly healthy when you are not just physically fit but also mentally and emotionally balanced. As Sri Sri Ravi Shankar puts it, "Health is not a mere absence of disease. It is a dynamic expression of life - in terms of how joyful, loving and enthusiastic you are." This is where yoga helps: postures, pranayama (breathing techniques) and meditation are a holistic fitness package.

Yoga-My personal fitness mantra,
My weight-loss formula,
My mind soother
My tool for better communication
My creativity machine
My doubt repeller My time planner

2 **Weight loss.** What many want! Yoga benefits here too. Sun Salutations and Kapal Bhati pranayama are some ways to help lose weight with yoga. Moreover, with regular practice of yoga, we tend to become more sensitive to the kind of food our body asks for and when. This can also help keep a check on weight.

3 **Stress relief.** A few minutes of yoga during the day can be a great way to get rid of stress that accumulates daily - in both the body and mind. Yoga postures, pranayama and meditation are effective techniques to release stress. You can also experience how yoga helps de-tox the body and

de-stress the mind at the Sri Sri Yoga Level 2 Course.

4 **Inner peace.** We all love to visit peaceful, serene spots, rich in natural beauty. Little do we realize that peace can be found right within us and we can take a mini-vacation to experience this any time of the day! Benefit from a small holiday every day with yoga and meditation. Yoga is also one of the best ways to calm a disturbed mind.

5 **Improved immunity.** Our system is a seamless blend of the body, mind and spirit. An irregularity in the body affects the mind and similarly unpleasantness or restlessness in the mind can manifest as an ailment in the body. Yoga poses massage organs and strengthens muscles; breathing techniques and meditation release stress and improve immunity.

6 **Living with greater awareness.** The mind is constantly involved in activity - swinging from the past to the future - but never staying in the present. By simply being aware of this tendency of the mind, we can actually save ourselves from getting stressed or worked up and relax the mind. Yoga and pranayama help create that -awareness and bring the mind back to the present moment, where it can stay happy and focused.

7 **Better relationships.** Yoga can even help improve your relationship with your spouse, parents, friends or loved ones. A mind that is relaxed, happy and contented is better able to deal with sensitive relationship matters. Yoga and meditation work on keeping the mind happy and peaceful; benefit from the strengthened special bond you share with people close to you.

8 Increased energy. Do you feel completely drained out by the end of the day? Shuttling between multiple tasks through the day can sometimes be quite exhausting. A few minutes of yoga everyday provides the secret to feeling

fresh and energetic even after a long day. A 10-minute online guided meditation benefits you immensely, leaving you refreshed and recharged in the middle of a hectic day.

9 Better flexibility and posture. You only need to include yoga in your daily routine to benefit from a body that is strong, supple and flexible. Regular yoga practice stretches and tones the body muscles and also makes them strong. It also helps improve your body posture when you stand, sit, sleep or walk. This would, in turn, help relieve you of body pain due to incorrect posture.

10 Better intuition. Yoga and meditation have the power to improve your intuitive ability so that you effortlessly realize what needs to be done, when and how, to yield positive results. It works. You only need to experience it yourself. Remember, yoga is a continuous process. So keep practicing! The deeper you move into your yoga practice, the more profound are its benefits.

MEANING- DEFINITION AND PRINCIPLES OF RECREATION

Recreation is an activity of leisure, leisure being discretionary time. The "need to do something for recreation" is an essential element of human biology and psychology. Recreational activities are often done for enjoyment, amusement, or pleasure and are considered to be "fun".

Definition of Recreation

There is some consensus on the definition of recreation. Recreation is an activity that people engage in during their free time, that people enjoy, and that people recognize as having socially redeeming values. Unlike leisure, recreation has a connotation of being morally acceptable not just to the individual

but also to society as a whole, and thus we program for

those activities within that context. While recreation activities can take many forms, they must contribute to society in a way that society deems acceptable. This means that activities deemed socially acceptable for recreation can change over time.

Examples of recreational activities are endless and include sports, music, games, travel, reading, arts and crafts, and dance. The specific activity performed is less important than the reason for performing the activity, which is the outcome. For most the desired outcome is recreation or restoration. Participants hope that their recreation pursuits can help them to balance their lives and refresh themselves from their work as well as other mandated activities such as housecleaning, child rearing, and so on.

People also see recreation as a social instrument because of its contribution to society. That is, professionals have long used recreation programs and services to produce socially desirable outcomes, such as the wise use of free time, physical fitness, and positive youth development. The organized development of recreation programs to meet a variety of physical, psychological, and social needs has led to recreation playing a role as a social instrument for well-being and, in some cases, change. This role has been the impetus for the development of many recreation providers from municipalities to non-profits such as the YMCA, and YWCA. There are also for-profit agencies, such as fitness centres and spas, designed to provide positive outcomes.

Principles of Recreation

There are many principles of recreation that exist in the world. And some of them are quite easily applicable to both children and adults. There are new forms of recreation available today.

1) Every child needs to be exposed to the growth giving activities that have brought satisfaction through the

ages - from climbing, chasing, tumbling; to tramping, swimming, dancing, skating, ball games; to singing, playing musical instruments, dramatizing; to making things with his hands, to working with sticks and stones and sand and water, to building and modelling; to caring for pets; to gardening, to nature; to trying simple scientific experiments; to learning team play, group activity and adventure and comradeship in doing things with others.

2) Every child needs to discover which activities give him personal satisfaction. In these activities he should be helped to develop the essential skills. Several of these activities should be of such a nature that he can keep them up in adult life.
3) Every man should have certain forms of recreation which require little space and which can be fitted into small fragments of time.
4) Every man needs to know well a certain limited number of indoor and outdoor games which he himself likes so that there will never be an occasion when he cannot think of anything to do.
5) Everyone should form a habit of reading.
6) Most people should know at least a few songs with good music so that they may sing when they feel like it.
7) Everyone should be helped to learn how to make something of beauty in line, form, colour, sound, or the graceful use of his own body. At least he should find pleasure in what others do in painting, woodworking, sculpture, photography, if he cannot himself use these forms of expression.
8) Everyone should be helped to form habits of being active, of breathing deeply in the sunlit outdoor air. Man thrives best in the sunlight. Since living, not business, is the end of life, our cities should be planned for living as well as for

business and industry. Sunlight, air, open spaces, parks, playgrounds, in abundant measure are essential to any living that is to give permanent satisfaction.

9) Every man should be encouraged to find one or more hobbies.
10) It is of the greatest importance that every person be exposed to rhythm because without rhythm man is incomplete.
11) About one year in every ten of a man's life is spent in eating. It is of fundamental importance that this one-tenth of a man's life shall be so lit up by play of mind upon mind that eating shall not be a hurried chore but an opportunity for comradeship and for growth for the whole man. Eating should be a social occasion, in the home something of a ceremony.
12) Rest, repose, reflection, contemplation are in themselves a form of recreation and ought never to be crowded out by more active play.
13) Those recreational activities are most important which most completely command the individual so that he loses himself in them and gives all that he has and is to them.
14) Ultimate satisfaction in recreation comes only through one's own achievement of some kind.
15) The form of one's recreation as an adult often, though not always, should be such as to use in part powers unused in the rest of one's life.
16) A man is successful in his recreational life in so far as the forms of activity he chooses create a play spirit, a humour, which to some extent pervades all his working hours, helping him to find enjoyment constantly in the little events of life.
17) The happy play of childhood is essential to normal growth. Normal men are most likely to grow from the children who have played well and happily. Normal men more

easily continue normally as they keep up childhood habits of play.

18) Participation as a citizen in the cooperative building of a better way of life in which all may share is one of the most permanently satisfying forms of recreation.

19) That children and men and women may be more likely to live this kind of life, experience shows there is need for community action:

- Every community needs a person, and an unpaid committee or board charged with thinking, planning, and working to provide opportunity for the best possible use of the leisure hours of men, women, and children.
- Community recreation programs should continue throughout the year
- Support of community recreation programs should be through tax funds under some department of the local government.
- Every community needs playgrounds, parks, and recreation centres just as every city and town needs streets and sewers.
- Every community should provide opportunity for the children when they leave school to continue the musical and dramatic and other specialized recreation activities which they have enjoyed during school days.
- Community recreation programs should allow for a broad range of tastes and interests and varying degrees of mental and physical energy.
- Every community needs persons trained to lead in recreation just as much as it needs persons trained in education.
- Satisfying recreation, whether for the individual or for the community, involves careful planning.

Role of recreation in promoting Physical Education

- Proximity of Facilities: It has been demonstrated that parks, recreation, fitness and sport facilities within close proximity to one's home often mean that citizens engage in more physical activity. The closer the facility/ program, the more likely it is that a resident will make use of it. Studies demonstrated that there were differences even between distances as small as one mile and one half mile with those in close walking distance. The socio-economic status (SES) of neighbourhoods often dictates what physical activity resources are available and how accessible they are to the residents. Individuals from lower SES neighbourhoods may have limited ability to control their physical activity in the face of Inaccessible environments.
- The Great Outdoors and Physical Activity
- Outdoor recreation and access to nature play a vital role in the physical, psychological, spiritual well-being, health, and development of people of all ages. Open space and outdoor recreation areas provide places for people to play and exercise. Activity such as this contributes to public health and can also help reduce health care costs. Outdoor recreation activities that enhance health and wellness, however many of these do not have easy access to majority of cities and large

urban areas. Urban parks and community green spaces are essential to providing places for people to enjoy recreation outdoors. In addition to federally owned and operated lands, state, county, and municipal entities manage thousands of parks, natural areas, and historic sites that can provide countless opportunities for physical activity. Linking Sports with Community Physical activity, there are a wide variety of professional, amateur (AAU Olympics) and college athletic and sports facilities throughout the country that are utilized by athletes training at an elite level. These same facilities could be used to enhance physical activity opportunities in communities without subtracting from their primary uses. This would increase the number of available facilities in a dense area with little room for new building and allow for shared resources in a world where duplication is becoming increasingly costly and wasteful.

MISCONCEPTIONS ABOUT YOGA AND DIFFERENCE BETWEEN YOGA & NON YOGIC EXERCISE

Although the practice of yoga has become widespread over the last 30 years, there are still quite a few misconceptions about this ancient method of self-transformation. Here is a brief survey of the most common myths about yoga, and a look at what yoga is really all about.

1 **Yoga is a sport:** One of the important components of yoga is the practice of physical postures, known as asanas in Sanskrit. Due to this physical aspect of yoga, some people think of yoga as a sport or an activity akin to body building. In this sense, yoga is seen as a casual pastime which one can take up and practice now and then like any sport. The fact is that yoga is the art and the science of physical, mental and spiritual development. Although the yoga postures may look like the stretching exercises found in some sports. The exercises in yoga are one part of an all-around program of personal development. The postures are not an end in themselves, but are meant to help prepare one's body for mental and spiritual development.

2 **The physical side of yoga is the most important part:** Although the practice of yoga postures is the most commonly known aspect of yoga, it is not the most

important part. In fact, the ancient system of yoga begins with the understanding and practice of moral precepts and living a life in harmony with self and society. The foundation of yoga lies on the observance of principles such as not harming others, acting in the spirit of welfare, non-stealing, non-accumulation of excessive physical wealth, viewing all things as an expression of consciousness, purity of mind, contentment, and selfless service. If you can learn how to live in harmony with those around you, and at the same time work on your own inner development, then the other components of yoga (postures, concentration and meditation) can be practiced with the best possible effects.

3 **Yoga is only for women:** In some parts of the world the majority of yoga students are women, and some men may have gotten the idea that yoga is not for them. The fact is that all people are searching for inner peace and all people wish to avoid disease and live a healthy life. Yoga offers something for anyone who wishes an effective method of physical, mental or spiritual development and should not be thought of as a discipline reserved only for women or only for men.

4 **Everybody must practice the same postures:** In most yoga classes around the world you will find that several people at a time are practicing the same postures. Despite this widespread convention, the needs of individuals vary according to their physical structures and it is best to perform yoga postures that are individually suited to a particular individual. For example, a young man suffering from asthma will need postures that are quite different from an older woman with heart problems. If you want to practice yoga postures correctly it is best to find a teacher who is able to prescribe

the postures that are best suited to your particular needs.

5 **You have to be extremely agile to practice yoga:** It is true that some yoga postures are a bit difficult to perform, and require an agile body. However, just as postures should be selected according to the ailments that a person suffers from, a good yoga instructor will be able to show you postures that are within your reach. When performing yoga postures, you should try to do them to the best of your ability and you shouldn't worry whether you look like the picture in the book. Often, just the effort that you make in trying to perform the posture is enough to reap the benefits of that posture.

6 **It is good to practice yoga postures out of doors:** When you perform yoga properly your body becomes very sensitive to shifts in temperature. If you practice outside your house even a slight breeze may be enough to make you uncomfortable or even catch cold. It is best to practice indoors. The windows may be open but you should stay away from drafts. In summer it is best to turn off fans while practicing yoga postures.

7 **Incense should be burned when practicing yoga:** Although yoga comes from India, and so does much of the world's incense, it is not a good idea to burn incense while performing yoga postures or doing meditation. Yoga postures should be done in a smoke-free area: this includes cigarette smoke and also the smoke of incense. During meditation the smoke of burning incense will cause disturbance and hinder the process of going within. Incense can be used before doing meditation or before practicing postures in order to create a nice atmosphere, but there should not be smoke in the air when the actual practice begins. If you practice yoga regularly and do so with a proper understanding of its

holistic nature, you will surely realize great benefits in all spheres of life.

Difference between Yoga and Non Yogic Exercise

Every beginner who is interested to start practicing Yoga, should check out these differences.

Yoga and exercises both have their own purpose to be performed. The basic differences between yoga and exercise are: Yoga can make your body, mind and soul calm, but exercise can't do anything to your mind and soul, it will strength and shape your body.

The respiration rate falls in yogic exercises as they are done slowly. In physical exercises, respiratory system is made to work hard as they are done quickly.

The temperature falls down in yoga whereas physical exercises increase the temperature of body.

The metabolic rate will be less in practicing yogic exercises whereas it is increased in physical exercises hence yoga practitioners require less food than people practicing physical exercising.

Yogic exercise activates the parasympathetic nervous system while physical exercise activates the sympathetic nervous system. Yogic exercises develop flexibility and the ability to adapt to new environments if practiced correctly and they help in developing stamina.

Yogic exercises help to coordinate the endocrinal secretions and balancing the reactions and develop a positive attitude in life.

Physical exercises develop toxins whereas yogic exercises help in removing them.

The results of yoga may be slow, but they have long-term benefits compared to exercises.

About the Author

Padmakshan Padmanabhan has been involved in physical education, training, adventure activities and coaching for the past twenty-six years. He was former Chief Physical Training Instructor of the Indian Navy and has had considerable experience in the field of Sports and physical Education. He served as a Senior Physical Training Instructor at various Armed Forces Training Institutes including the Indian Navy Physical Training School—the premier Trainer's Training School of the Indian Navy. He completed his post-graduation in Sports Management from Alagappa University and Physical Trainer, First Class, course from Indian Armed Forces (Indian Navy). He also underwent various courses in physical training and sports medicine at the Indian Armed Forces Sports Medicine Centre–Pune, Sports Authority of India`s National Institute of Sports and National Institute of Water Sports.

A former national level volleyball player and a certified coach from the National Institute of Sports, he also played water polo at various levels and has expertise in aqua training and physical conditioning. He has wide knowledge and experience in the field of physical training, education, coaching, sports medicine, fitness and the Yogic method of physical well-being. He has attended several national and international seminars. He played a crucial role as an official in organizing the World Military Games in 2007 at Hyderabad, Commonwealth Youth Games at Pune and Commonwealth Games at Delhi. He is currently the Director of Sports with Mahatma Education Society's Pillai Group of Institutions at Mumbai.

The Mahatma Education Society (MES) was founded in 1970 and the Pillai Group has been into education since its inception. Today the Group runs 48 institutions in and around Mumbai.

Sophisticated training facilities, state of the art equipment, a dynamic reach in faculty make the institutions of the Pillai Group some of the most sought after in Mumbai.

MES also has international exchange programmes with some of the leading educational institutions abroad. Today the Pillai Group of International schools and colleges enjoys the highest rankings at the state, national and international levels.

"Education for All" is the founder CEO's dream. And he is on his way to fulfilling it.

About Indus Source Books

Indus Source Books is a niche, independent book publisher in Mumbai passionately committed to publishing good and relevant literature. We believe that books are one of the most important mediums of communication and we seek to bring out publications that help to serve the community and the world we live in.

At Indus Source Books, we celebrate the diverse spiritual traditions, culture, and history of the world and present it to our readers in a contemporary format that retains its essential flavour: "Indian Spirit, Universal Wisdom".

Visit our website www.indussource.com for more details.

Indus Source Books
PO Box 6194
Malabar Hill PO
Mumbai 400006
India
www.indussource.com
info@indussource.com